THE OLD AND NEW TESTAMENTS

FAITH AND SCHOLARSHIP
COLLOQUIES SERIES

What Has Archaeology To Do with Faith?
The Old and New Testaments

THE OLD AND NEW TESTAMENTS

Their Relationship
and the "Intertestamental" Literature

Edited by
James H. Charlesworth and
Walter P. Weaver

Faith and Scholarship Colloquies

Trinity Press International   Valley Forge, Pa.

First Edition 1993

Trinity Press International
P.O. Box 851
Valley Forge, PA 19482-0851

Cover design by Jim Gerhard

Library of Congress Cataloging-in-Publication Data

The Old and New Testaments : their relationship and the
    "intertestamental" literature / edited by James H. Charlesworth and
    Walter P. Weaver. — 1st ed.
        p.   cm. — (Faith and scholarship colloquies)
    Includes bibliographical references and index.
    ISBN 1-56338-062-5
    1. Bible.   N.T.—Relation to the Old Testament.   2. Apocryphal
books—Criticism, interpretation, etc.   3. Judaism—History—Post-
exilic period, 586 B.C.-210 A.D.   4. Judaism—Relations—
Christianity.   5. Christianity and other religions—Judaism.
I. Charlesworth, James H.   II. Weaver, Walter P.   III. Series.
BS2387.043   1993
220.6—dc20   93-31235
                                                                        CIP

Printed in the United States of America.

93 94 95 96 97 98   6 5 4 3 2 1

This book is for
HUGH ANDERSON
Peerless Scholar
Continuing Mentor
and
Gracious Friend
who also
Strikes the wee ball well

CONTENTS

CONTRIBUTORS

Bernhard W. Anderson is Professor of Old Testament Theology Emeritus at Princeton Theological Seminary and currently Adjunct Professor of Old Testament in the Boston University Theological School.

John J. Carey is Chairman of the Department of Religion and Professor at Agnes Scott College in Decatur, Ga. He held the Pendergrass Chair in Religion at Florida Southern College, Lakeland, in the 1988–89 academic year.

James H. Charlesworth is George L. Collord Professor of New Testament Language and Literature at Princeton Theological Seminary and director of the Princeton Theological Seminary Dead Sea Scrolls Project.

R. Frank Johnson is Professor of Religion and Philosophy at Florida Southern College, Lakeland.

Walter P. Weaver is Chairman of the Humanities Division and the Department of Religion and Philosophy at Florida Southern College, Lakeland, and is its Pendergrass Professor of Religion.

Faith and Scholarship Colloquies

This series explores the boundaries where faith and academic study intersect. At these borders, the sharp edge of current biblical scholarship is allowed to cut theologically and pose its often challenging questions for traditional faith. The series includes contributions from leading scholars in contemporary biblical studies. As Christian faith seeks to speak a word in our day that is as powerful as those in the past, it needs to sharpen its perception and proclamation with the help of honest and truthful insights in human knowledge, ranging from first-century archaeology to modern linguistics.

Preface

Christians are concerned to know how, if at all, the New Testament is related to the Old Testament. Why are religious services organized so that there are readings from the Old and New Testaments?

Ministers are perplexed by the Bible and are often tempted to base their sermons on some contemporary event or on a well-known novel. What impact has a two-thousand-year-old book, or collection of books, on modern problems?

How is one to preach from the Old and the New Testaments? How are the Testaments related? While ministers know that the New Testament authors claimed that Jesus was the Christ prophesied by the prophets, they also perceive there is a sense in which those same authors suggest that his coming did not fulfill God's promises. The heathen and idolatrous nations were not driven from Jerusalem. The lion did not begin to lie down with the lamb. Peace was not observed on God's holy mountain. In fact, just forty years after Jesus' crucifixion the Romans burned the Temple in Jerusalem and brought to an end the history of ancient Israel.

Having been taught in many seminaries and universities that the Testaments cannot simply be related in terms of promise and fulfillment, ministers want to know how this paradigm can be used today. Are the Testaments related in terms of God's covenant in the way Walther Eichrodt thought in the 1930s? Is there a development of certain basic ideas, such as kingship, election, and covenant, as many biblical experts have claimed? Was Rudolf Bultmann right that the Old Testament reveals a history of failure?

Is the Bible the paradigm for Christian belief? Are we left to confess in mutually idiosyncratic ways that God has spoken individually to us in ways that help us to relate the Testaments but that do not clarify how we do so? Should we display our Bibles as models of what we cherish but nonetheless as books that we do not read? If we read them, are they to be interpreted by the guidance of the Spirit and not an educated intellect? What relevance has scholarship for faith?

These concerns were considered to be so significant and widely recognized that Florida Southern College organized a symposium to address them. The resulting lectures now appear here in print.

A major development since the discussion of these issues in the sixties by Bernhard W. Anderson, Rudolf Bultmann, Walther Eichrodt, Gerhard von Rad, and others is the prominence now being given to the Pseudepigrapha and related literatures. One of the missing links that will help us rearticulate the issues and attempt to discern how the Christian's Testaments are related is the abundance of so-called intertestamental literature now available and the recognition that the Jewish writings in the Pseudepigrapha and the Dead Sea Scrolls are significant documents that were considered by many Jews, including some of Jesus' followers, to have been inspired.

These early Jewish writings date from the centuries that separate, for example, Daniel from Revelation. They help bridge the alleged chasm from the earliest book in the Old Testament to the oldest book in the New Testament, or from Daniel in c. 165 B.C.E. to 1 Thessalonians in c. 50 C.E.

Some of the comments published during the earlier

decades when a discussion of the relation of the Testaments was in vogue, especially before the forties in Germany, would be branded today as blatantly anti-Semitic (or anti-Jewish). Some of the words used by Bultmann, for example, are no longer possible in today's pluralistic society and in light of our appreciation of the continuing covenant between God and the Jews. Today the discussion of the relation of the Testaments is related to a parallel concern—to seek to find ways to celebrate the similarities and also the differences among Jews and Christians, the two sisters of the Judaism of Jesus' day.

Although these essays are addressed primarily to Christians, they are published with the recognition that scholarly attempts to clarify issues of faith must be done not only in a parochial setting but also before others of different faiths and commitments. We recognize that our thoughts must be defensible within our own faith communities, but they must also be recognized as viable perspectives to others.

James H. Charlesworth

Acknowledgments

A number of persons needs to be acknowledged for the preparation of this volume. First, thanks go to the members of the symposium. Their work deserves a wider audience.

Second, thanks also go to Florida Southern College for hosting an annual biblical seminar designed to explore issues of current significance for ministers, scholars, students, faculty, and laypersons. The president of Florida Southern, Dr. Robert A. Davis, has given vigorous support to this enterprise.

The management of the symposium was undertaken by the members of the Department of Religion and Philosophy at Florida Southern College, whose otherwise unrecognized efforts made all things operate smoothly. A word of thanks is due the secretary of the department, Mrs. Beverly Johnson, for meritorious service in the preparation of these manuscripts and other works in the planning and conduct of the symposium.

A word of thanks is extended to Princeton Theological Seminary for assistance in preparing the final draft of this volume. Professor Patrick Miller, and Graduate Assistants Mark Harding, David Freedholm, and Loren Shickenbrack deserve our special appreciation.

Introduction

Walter P. Weaver

Why would anyone want to take up anew the question of the relationship of the Old and New Testaments? It is, after all, an ancient question with a seemingly fixed range of answers and no new solutions to be posed. Yet circumstances do change and force a reconsideration of old issues. It is also true that some questions require renewal from time to time simply because their importance imposes itself upon us. Although the latter assuredly applies to the subject before us, we ought primarily to take note of the circumstances that generally prevail today, circumstances that suggest that a reconsideration of the issue of the relationship of the Testaments is timely.

A Range of Circumstances

Among the current circumstances, we may notice a recurrence of anti-Semitism. Although happening apparently at the fringes of our society, anti-Semitism is never to be dismissed casually as merely the lunatic rumblings of disoriented minds. Wherever it appears it is threatening, and not merely to Jews. It represents a blot on the human story, and its ultimate end is holocaust. It must not be allowed to come among us again. Its apparent infection in the youth of the country makes all the more urgent some countervailing forces. In this light it remains continually important to refocus the question of the relationship of the Testaments and how the two communities—Jews and Christians—are connected with one another. Not to face the question is to risk objectifying one another out of ignorance; this situation, from either end, leads to darkness and the possibility of racial harm.

A second consideration arises from the Christian side and has to do with the renewed appropriation of "Israel" by the religious right. It is of course true that the Christian community generally has always appropriated Israel as its own—in what legitimate sense is partly the subject of these essays—but also there is a special claim entered by the religious fundamentalists in America. Especially, apocalyptic fundamentalism tends to hinge its eschatological expectations on certain Old Testament texts and in particular on the doings of the modern state of Israel. The restoration of Israel has come to be a significant element in expectation of the Parousia of Jesus; an extension of that belief is the contention that the Temple will soon be restored in Jerusalem, signifying the approach of the end. These beliefs contain the tacit assumption that the modern state of Israel is essentially continuous with ancient Israel.

A third characteristic of the present period of studying the relation of the Testaments is the innovation introduced by modern and secular biblical scholarship. There are Christian scholars of the Old Testament, and there are also Jewish scholars who have mastered the New Testament. In addition, the scholarly community does not rely on faith commitments in order to carry out its scholarship. No one, in fact, has to be a committed believer of any sort in order to be a scholar of the Bible. All biblical historians of whatever persuasion personally share a common methodology. Historical criticism is in reality a child of the Enlightenment, as is scientific thought generally; its assumptions are not those of faith, but those of reason and its attempts at "objective" and inductive examination. The scholarly community may and does consist of all sorts of individuals with agendas quite different in nature and scope. The Jew and the Christian may and often do labor side by side in the study of texts; they share a common hope of new knowledge and understanding. This scholarship is something new in the history of Jewish and Christian relations, and it injects a different element into the discussion. It makes possible a dialogue on biblical texts, creating a kind of community of scholars even where the theological questions are muted, as they often must be in order to carry forth the scholarly task. Yet such questions lie close at hand, and it is the purpose of this volume to explore them.

At the same time, we need not obscure the fact that even scholarship may have hidden agendas that are not so evident through the layer of objectivity laid over them. Consider, for example, the form-critical study of the historical Jesus. Ostensibly, the method called *Formgeschichte* was developed to understand better the processes of oral tradition, with the special goal of reaching back to the oldest "layer" of Jesus-tradition, thereby coming nearer to the historical Jesus himself. Among the prominent criteria for deciding which texts were traceable to Jesus was the general rule that nothing could be ascribed to Jesus that showed influence from either the Easter faith or Judaism. Jesus was not allowed to be either a Christian or a Jew. The obvious intention of such a severe rule was to establish the uniqueness of Jesus' message over against his immediate environment. But precisely here serious questions arise: Is there not something suspect about this desire on the part of supposedly objective historians to paint a picture of a "unique" Jesus, especially one who stands out from his Judaic background? Uniqueness is a category in which historians ought not to traffic; it seems to conceal some theological assumptions about the nature of Jesus of Nazareth. The motive in such rule making may not necessarily be anti-Semitic, but Jewish scholars might be forgiven if they feel a bit of a sting in this alleged scholarly generalization. So the question of the relation of the Testaments again begs for a hearing, and it requires us always to be vigilant that even scholarship itself is not subverted into an instrument of apologetics or propaganda.[1]

A fourth consideration relates to the continued use of the Old Testament by the Christian community. This use occurs in a variety of ways, and it is characteristic that not even Christians agree among themselves as to the proper approach to the Old Testament. On the one hand are the religious fundamentalists who transfer texts from the Old Testament into the current scene and use them as though they were immediately authoritative. Even in nonfundamentalist circles, the text often is employed in a similar way, if not literally then at least normatively. An example might be the Ten Commandments, commonly cited in Christian churches as the epitome of the Christian ethic. This continuing hermeneutical appropriation of the Old Testament text within the Christian community raises theological issues to which we must still address ourselves.

A fifth consideration in the contemporary setting is the ongoing pluralism of Western society and its implications for a relationship between the Jewish and Christian communities. It is certainly unpopular in Western society to take notice of religious differences, or at least to emphasize them. On the contrary, our pluralistic society devalues those differences and attempts to impose a kind of cultural oneness that masks theological disagreements. In such an environment it is all too easy to pretend that differences are not important, or that the commonalities overrule the oppositions. The historical Christian claim to exclusivity of salvation can scarcely be entered into the conversation. How is it possible in this setting to combine an exclusive claim with membership in a society that has devalued all such claims? Of course, that is a peculiarly Christian problem, or at least it is formulated in a peculiarly Christian way. As a Jewish problem, it might be said to relate to how the exclusive claim to be the covenant people can be reconciled with a culture whose values are rooted in a different assumption.

Finally, there is the rather obvious fact that two communities exist today that have a shared tradition and therefore are compelled by the very nature of their existence to have a conversation with one another. It may be argued that the problem is predominantly a Christian one, in that Christians claim Israel in a way in which it is impossible for Israel to claim Christians. That is certainly true, and in this sense the question of the relationship of the Testaments is a Christian problem. It is a Jewish problem in the broader sense that Jews have historically been compelled to find their identity, at least in the West, within a culture that has come, since the Constantinian settlement, to be dominated by the Christian perspective. Even Jewish values, as embodied in the Old Testament, have been transmitted to the dominant culture largely through the Christian community. So a certain amount of history is shared; certain ideas prevail in both communities, such as the basic conviction that revelation occurs in and through events, that certain moral imperatives are divinely given.

Nevertheless, this shared element ought not to obscure the discontinuities. It could even be said that there exists a commonality of interest, but hardly a *shared* history in a genuinely existential sense. Certainly for the first Christians the history was shared, but then they evidently did not see themselves cut off from Judaism. It was apparently Paul who first raised this question to the level of conscious reflection, as he shows in Romans 9–11 (without, we can add, seeing himself separated from Judaism). And still it is not really possible to appeal, say, to the authority of Matthew without also recognizing the bitter hostility exhibited there toward the synagogue; or similarly with the Gospel of John, where the "Jews" have virtually lost their historical identity and become symbols for rejection and unbelief.[2] The appeals to the Old Testament within the Christian community, therefore, always contain a kind of pathos and a danger; they are filled not only with continuity but with contradiction as well. (The pathos lies in the paradoxical use of a text from whose community the user has become alienated, whereas the danger resides in the hermeneutical misreading of that text from its own context.) From this perspective the "problem" of the relationship of the Testaments is exclusively a Christian problem. It is a problem for the Jewish community only because it is a problem for the Christian community.

Now, of course, it can be argued that the question we are here raising (relationship of the Testaments) can be pursued independently of the larger issue of the contemporary relationship of the Jewish and Christian communities. It is certainly possible to regard the issue of relationship as a historical-theological matter to be resolved within its own boundaries, whereas the question of the relatedness of two communities today is to be thought through on its own merits. There is something to be said for that; the relationship of the Testaments is a question of the connection between two *documents,* whereas the other matter has to do with the relationship between two sociological entities. This posture has all the more compelling ground when it is again recalled that modern, secular Israel is no more continuous with ancient religious Israel than is the contemporary church with the first disciples. Yet we are not only considering modern Israel, but contemporary Jews who claim an identity arising from the *Tanakh.* We are also including modern Christians who see that same ancient history as their history. So a relationship of some sort is unavoidable. There is also the common historical ground on which each group stands. And because in both communities the historical so obviously becomes entangled with the theological, we must inevitably speak about the latter.

Persistent Themes

A number of significant issues have appeared not only in the essays included in this volume but in the discussions that followed their presentation in the symposium. These issues can be encapsulated as follows, with reference especially to the lively conversation among the panelists.

Hermeneutical Issues: The Noncanonical Works

It was widely agreed that there is no passage from the Old to the New Testament that does not navigate through the pseudepigraphical and apocryphal waters. Without these works the connection is broken. It is not merely a question of antecedent and consequence, or of getting some illuminating information about the New Testament background, but of understanding how two existing communities can appropriate the same traditions in such diverse ways. Both the synagogue and the church emerged out of a common tradition; one went off into the New Testament, the other into the Mishnah and Talmud. Yet both claim the same roots. The only way to grasp such phenomena as a precondition of further conversation is first to dig in the soil from which each sprang. We may take as an example the discussion that was aroused by Frank Johnson's analysis of the servant texts in Deutero-Isaiah. His characterization of the kerygmatic appropriation of those texts within the early Christian community raised the question of an existing suffering messianic expectation within Judaism. The comments of James Charlesworth are instructive:

> Did the earliest followers of Jesus and the authors of the New Testament see him as the suffering servant? The answer is emphatically yes. Did Early Judaism have the concept of a suffering servant? The answer is emphatically no. Did some of the authors of the Old Testament look for an eschatological "messiah"? The answer is probably not.

In the Old Testament, "messiah" is used, as we all know, primarily for the king, sometimes for the prophet, and infrequently for the priest. But we look in vain for the expectation of "the messiah" who will come. On the other hand, there are many messianic ideas. These are in the air, but it wasn't until later that the movement from messianic ideas to proclamation and expectation of the messiah occurs. It begins to appear very clearly in the first century B.C.E.

Every text that we have to work with that refers to the messiah as a figure dates after Daniel, or c. 165 B.C.E. We have so many confluences, so many living, rich traditions, all of which are, in my estimation, by the first century highly apocalyptic and eschatological. And what is now becoming clear is that some of them are being united. A striking variety appears, such as messiah, suffering one, suffering servant, righteous one, son of man. What is really very exciting is that we find the messiah, the righteous one, and the son of man in 1 Enoch 37–71. Almost everyone now recognizes that this material is probably pre–70 and Jewish. And if in fact the parables of Enoch are indeed Jewish, Palestinian, and somewhat contemporaneous with Jesus, how are the messiah, the righteous one, and the son of man related? They seem to be not only terms but titles, and most of us are arguing now that these are related. This is like a quantum leap. If indeed we have here the mentality of a Jewish group, then we are beginning to see behind the movement that we call the Palestinian Jesus Movement. We are finding other Palestinian movements going in this direction, bringing together a lot of these traditions that we had argued incorrectly must be separated.

In addressing the question whether the Dead Sea Scrolls characterized the Righteous Teacher, the founder of the community, in similar ways, Charlesworth observed:

> If you look at the concept of suffering and the concept of "messiah" in the Dead Sea Scrolls, you are not going to find linking as far as I see. The Righteous Teacher, I think, did clearly see himself as the suffering one, as "the poor one." He was the suffering one, and he urged his disciples, his followers, to see themselves as the poor ones. But the messiah was never associated with the Righteous Teacher.

It is quite clear, however, that the early Christian community saw Jesus in this way and regarded his suffering death as efficacious. But the problem remains how that community managed to seize upon the notion that Jesus was both the sufferer and the messiah. Again, Charlesworth commented:

> How could they make this argument? They can put forth the argument that he was the servant who was to suffer. But how could they make the argument that he was "the messiah"? Only by linking the messiah with the servant. Then the question becomes, Could they legitimately do that? The question that we still cannot answer is why the earliest followers of Jesus chose the title "messiah" and called him Jesus Christ when so many other titles and terms would have been so much easier—righteous one, for example. Clearly, that would have been easy, and there are other people who make that move. It is made in 1 Enoch 37–71; it is clearly made in the Odes of Solomon; and it is hinted in the Gospel of John. But why the Christ? Why the messiah? Jesus does not fulfill anything that we find in Jewish sources; he does not drive out the Gentiles; he dies. The only passage in Jewish literature—except for the late medieval literature, in which the messiah is to die—is in 4 Ezra. And that, of course, is also post—70, and the messiah's death means nothing; it is nonefficacious. He just simply dies, and those who are with him die.

Charlesworth went on to suggest a possible answer to his own question—that the messianic title for Jesus arose out of the polemical situation of the early community; that is, it was a response to the community's accusers who denigrated their faith in Jesus. As Charlesworth put it, "Maybe the title "messiah" was thrust upon them as a rejection and as a curse."

However such matters may finally be resolved, if at all, it is immediately apparent that the issue of relating two Testaments cannot be divorced from the insistence on a grounding in the intervening, noncanonical literature. A theological answer has to be preceded by historical understanding. The question with which we began discloses itself as a hermeneutical issue of diverse dimension, the first element of which requires some grasp of the existence of two historical communities interpreting common traditions in unique ways.

Hermeneutical Issues: Canonical Criticism

If it is necessary to urge an expansion of the historical horizons in debating the relationship of the Testaments, then the question also presses as to the significance of the limits of the traditional canon. Whereas Charlesworth, in his essay, examined the thesis of Brevard Childs with some critical commentary, Bernhard Anderson, in his reaction to the Johnson essay, insisted somewhat more positively on reading texts within the given canonical setting. He remarked:

> The question I would raise is whether we need even to go beyond stylistic criticism and to consider the function of that poem, not only in the poems of so-called Second Isaiah, but in the larger Book of Isaiah itself, that is to say, the canonical whole. If you look at the poem within the structure of Isaiah 40–55, you may raise the question as to whether those songs really have a separate identity, whether they can be torn from the texture of the poetry itself. It is my own view that the Book of Isaiah in its final form, in its redacted form, displays the outlook, the perspective, of an apocalyptic community. The whole Isaianic tradition has been reread from the standpoint of apocalyptic theology. If that is the case, then you have to discuss the role of these poems, the function of these poems, in that larger whole. And I would think that the final apocalyptic rereading of the Book of Isaiah would bring us very close to the New Testament. It certainly would bring us very close to the community of Qumran, where Scripture functioned in an apocalyptic worldview. So I would think one of the questions for fruitful exploration would be how this portrait of the servant of God functions in the whole canonical structure of the Book of Isaiah, and especially in an apocalyptic framework or mentality.

Although Anderson did not elaborate on what such an apocalyptic reading of Isaiah might look like, he gave some indication of its direction when reflecting on the apocalyptic interpretation of the Righteous Teacher at Qumran, and of Jesus of Nazareth in early Christianity as well.

> I would think that the Righteous Teacher would have experienced suffering at the hands of the powers that be, and those powers could manifest themselves economically, politically, in terms of outright military action, or whatever. But in the apocalyptic mode of thinking, the powers that be are all a part of this present age, which is corrupt right to the core. And that age has to be changed. So the poor in that context would be those people who were victimized by the powers that be. I think in the apocalyptic rereading of the Isaiah tradition you would find that motif. In the eschatological day, the day of the coming of God's kingdom or God's reign, Jerusalem will be at the very center; it is there that the poor will experience their justice, their vindication. Whoever these poor are is very vague, but we know only that they are the poor who are victims, victims of power. And thus apocalyptic theology is trying to come to terms with violence, with power that is manifest not just in the heart, but out there at work in society, and that is manifest now in the powers that be. And then the question is, Was Jesus' suffering understood, apocalyptically, as being the kind of suffering that is imposed by these powers that be? Was his suffering then—and perhaps this goes completely beyond Qumran eschatologically—and certainly his vindication, regarded as the sign that the New Age is not only at hand, but actually entering into human history?

Such questioning sets out from the canonical literature, moves on through the vastness of the intertestamental works, and once again alights within the canon. And indeed the canon itself seems to justify such a journey, as when Jude in the New Testament quotes from the Book of Enoch authoritatively. Canonical criticism forces the issue of interpretation within the limits prescribed by synagogue and church, though such interpretation is only one level within a complex interrelationship of interpretations. What is now more clearly seen is the necessity of setting forth a history of interpretive traditions in order to locate the focus of one's interest (e.g., the suffering servant) along the spectrum of historical-communal hermeneutical experience.

Apocalypticism, Apocalyptic Writing and Thinking

The apocalyptic rereading of the Isaianic tradition proposed by Bernhard Anderson leads to a still larger consideration—the evaluation of apocalypticism generally as one of the "bridges" between the Testaments. The essay by John Carey especially focused on the validity of apocalyptic as a mode of thought, with Carey's own assessment somewhat negative on balance. The critical burden of his essay lay in his suspicion of the exclusivism of apocalyptic thought as an inappropriate mode of theological thought in the world today. It is so for a number of reasons, but especially in a pluralistic world that has increasingly negated all exclusivistic claims. This verdict over apocalyptic ways of thinking is basically negative, although in a reverse sense the positive conclusion can be drawn that an ecumenical, open dialogue with other faiths cannot be sustained from an apocalyptic point of view. If such a dialogue is mandatory or even merely desirable in the modern world, some other basis will have to be found.

Of course, it can also be said that the impulse toward some such transcendent conversation is itself born of the rationalistic period of human history; it does not necessarily derive from either the Old or the New Testament. Perhaps we are only imagining that our modern desires need to have some justification in the ancient, authoritative traditions. All of that may actually seem a bit strange, when the modern era itself has relativized those same authorities. In any case, Carey's work puts to us these very questions in a particularly pungent way.

There are also other evaluations of apocalypticism, and we might have expected that Anderson would reflect a somewhat different perspective:

As I read apocalyptic literature, it is not just exclusivistic, but is governed by a fundamental, universal perspective. In a profound sense apocalyptic represents a kind of new theology of creation, a theology that bursts beyond the limitations of the old prophetic framework, which was based too much upon the doctrine of sin and retribution, into a much larger vision of the enthronement of God as cosmic king and creator, not only over Israel, but over all of the nations.

As I see the apocalyptic vision, it has a strange combination—if not tension—between universalism and particularism. Apocalyptic theology with all its universalism, never surrenders the centrality of Zion, the centrality of the city of God.

Anderson then raised the further question of how early Christianity might have modified apocalyptic thinking, and offered the following proposition:

In my judgment, it is true to follow Käsemann and say that apocalypticism was the mother of all early Christian theology. I would be willing to defend the thesis that Christianity, in its earliest form, was apocalyptic in character, and even go beyond that and say that Jesus himself was an apocalyptic visionary. But granting all of that, the fundamental question is what change Christianity has brought about in the apocalyptic mentality or framework. And surely one of the fundamental changes is that the Christian gospel breaks with the dualism of apocalyptic, that is, the distinction between the present evil age and the age to come. Surely any reading of the New Testament would be sufficient to remind us that the heart of the Christian gospel is that the New Age has already begun to dawn in Jesus Christ, however that is expressed.

Charlesworth also expressed some misgivings with regard to the reading of apocalyptic literature that sees in it only a narrowly based view of the world and humankind.

In terms of apocalyptic dualism and the elitism which that creates, we have to go beyond that. But we need not strive to go beyond the dream that the apocalyptists had, that God has a message for all people, the disenfranchised and also the establishment.

Charlesworth also noticed some common misinterpreta-
tions of the apocalyptic writings that deserve some cor-
rection:

> If you read carefully through the apocalyptists' writings,
> they are making it very clear not to revolt, that the move-
> ment is from God's side. And if you look at the Psalms of
> Solomon 17–18, if you look at the Testament of Moses 11,
> the claim is, Do not drive the Gentiles out; that is God's
> doing.
> I think there is so much in the apocalyptic view. For
> example, the apocalyptists are the first in the whole his-
> tory of human letters to try to relate time, both protologi-
> cally and eschatologically. Second, the apocalyptists were
> the first ones to talk about a universal dimension and
> meaning to history, that it is not just linear, but teleologi-
> cal.

The debate will doubtless continue. Is apocalypticism
a viable bridge between the Testaments? Can it unite two
seemingly disparate communities? In this question all the
hermeneutical questions seem to merge: apocalypticism
was the ground in which early Christianity was planted;
at the same time it came forth from late Judaism and
therefore constituted a common resource of synagogue
and church. To access it historically we have to pass
through the apocryphal and pseudepigraphical literature
in which it has deposited itself. Thus a larger issue here
has developed than our symposium was made to serve.
And whether and how apocalypticism can continue to
supply a meaningful theological framework, a question
the Carey essay was originally designed to raise, remains
on the unfinished agenda of both Judaic and Christian
thought.

Models of Separation and Union

In his response to Bernhard Anderson's essay, Frank
Johnson touched on a persistent problem, in spite of the
evident good efforts to find ways of linking together the

Testaments. Speaking about the complex issue of framing an Old Testament theology so as to reflect some theological unity, he noted:

> One of the reasons for the traditional Jewish distrust of Old Testament theologies has been the way in which most, with the exceptions of von Rad and perhaps Eichrodt, of these theologies have been organized. They have been organized along lines that primarily use Christian categories of analysis. In other words, the very way they frame the questions dictates the kinds of answers that they get to the questions. And I'm wondering if one of the problems that Jewish scholars have had has been the way that we Christians have almost written them off, or cut them out of the dialogue, by the way in which we have set up the models to start with.

In response to further questions about the different ways in which the text of the Old Testament gets proclaimed in differing communities, Jewish and Christian, Johnson said:

> As I encounter the text, I encounter it as a Christian, not as a Jew. And I encounter the text already encumbered with the confession that the Christian community is trying to validate.

The problem of attempting to make some kind of hermeneutical abstraction from one's own theological confessions is obviously not new, and the necessity to de-absolutize one's own interpretive models would seem to be merely self-evident; but both always bear repetition. In this context John Carey observed:

> In my younger days I was more willing and able to talk about truth with a capital "T" than I am now. I think there are multiple truths and contextual truths and personal truths, and so on. I am reminded of an observation that I heard Richard Niebuhr make, lecturing to an ethics class, in which he observed that we can have notions of the absolute, but we have no absolute notions. And I think a lot of what has shaped so much of our Christian heritage is that we have assumed we had some absolute notions.

Bernhard Anderson also issued some appropriate warnings for anyone to observe when attempting to interpret material, such as the Old Testament, which still often remains alien to the modern interpreter:

> On the subject of the unity of the Old Testament, or even the unity of the Bible, I would think that that unity is not to be found in a theological concept. Perhaps that has been one of the errors we have made in the past; we have sought for some overarching concept or scheme. That, I think, is too rational, too logical an approach in dealing with this kind of literature, which is much more poetic. In dealing with material like this I think we have to avoid Western modes of conceptualization. We are going to have to be a little more biblical in our approach to the question of biblical theology.

Charlesworth broadly agreed, noting the universal human tendency to tell stories. It remains to be seen how the recognition of the narrative, storytelling, poetic character of biblical material will realize itself in construction of newer biblical theologies, and in particular of attempts to relate the two Testaments.

In the same vein there also emerged in discussion that item which continues to distinguish Christian belief, not only from the synagogue, but from many other religious traditions as well. That is Christian faith in the resurrection of Jesus. Anderson's essay pointed to the discontinuities between the Christian and Jewish communities; the focus of this discontinuity lies in the Christian assertion of Jesus' crucifixion-resurrection as salvific events. At the same time, this assertion itself is not without its own problematic, especially because "resurrection" is not something that normally lies within the province of the critical historian. As Anderson observed:

> I often wonder where, as a strict historian or critic, I am going to draw the line. I do not have any real clear answer to this except I do not see how Christianity could have emerged as such a powerful force in human history at that time, apart from such an experience of miracle.

Charlesworth agreed:

> There has to be an experience, and certainly we cannot force ourselves to describe in terms of physics what happened. But something was experienced, something profound on a continuum somewhere with what was really happening in the crucifixion.

At the same time, Charlesworth observed rightly that the "resurrection of the body after death was a very deep Jewish idea," and this observation makes it paradoxically clear that even the Christian faith in the resurrection of Jesus does not deliver us from sorting out the relationship of the two communities before us. For the Christian community could not even make its most special affirmation apart from antecedent roots in Judaism. Whether the concept of resurrection is dispensable, or at least reinterpretable in some other categories, is a particular problem for Christian thought today. It seems fair to note that, to this day at least, the Christian community seems little disposed to dispense with the category of "resurrection." Consequently, the linguistic connection to which the Charlesworth essay referred will likely continue and bear with it all its historic and knotty questions.

Notes

1. It is to be observed that the trend in Jesus research is away from this strict criterion and toward locating Jesus precisely within his Judaic context. See, for example, James H. Charlesworth, *Jesus Within Judaism: New Light from Exciting Archaeological Discoveries*, Anchor Bible Reference Library (New York: Doubleday, 1988), and E. P. Sanders, *Jesus and Judaism* (Philadelphia: Fortress Press, 1985).

2. Of course, it is also true that the Jewish sources, such as the Talmud, disclose another side of this same harsh debate. We are not making any point here about culpability, but merely observing a phenomenon.

1

The Bible as the Shared Story of a People

Bernhard W. Anderson

At the beginning of my teaching career, I gained a spurious reputation that has haunted me through the years. While teaching at Colgate University, I was invited to write an introduction to and commentary on the Book of Esther for *The Interpreter's Bible*. Somehow this project came to the attention of the editor of the student newspaper, and I was interviewed. Yes, I admitted, for *The Interpreter's Bible* I am writing on the Book of Esther, an exceptional piece of Scripture that does not mention God even once. Not long thereafter an article appeared in the student newspaper with the arresting headline: Dr. Anderson coauthor of Bible.

That initial scholarly assignment has had a profound influence upon my thinking through the years. For one thing, it introduced me to the mystery of "the eternal survival of the Jew," as Karl Barth put it; for the Book of Esther tells a story about Haman's attempt to execute Mordecai the Jew and even to liquidate the Jewish people in the Persian Empire. The story serves as the legend for Purim, a festival when the Jewish people, rejoicing in their survival after many pogroms, celebrate with great merriment and abandon, following the whimsical maxim "Drink wine until you can no longer tell the difference between blessed be Mordecai and cursed be Haman." The project also raised a question that has troubled Christians down through the centuries, that is, the relation between the Hebrew Bible (called the Old Testament in Christian circles) and the New Testament. Martin Luther, the leader of the Protestant Reformation, disliked the Book of Esther and wished that it were not included in the Christian Bible, for, he said, it is too Jewish and contains much worldly nonsense.

The Old Testament and Christian Faith

For many Christians today the Old Testament is a problem. It contains stories of violence that are too much like what we read in the daily newspapers. It contains many laws based on the distinction between clean and unclean, regulations about sacrifices to be carried out at the Temple, and dreary genealogies and ancient history. The attitude of many of us people is expressed in the story about the Sunday School teacher who, when dealing with the wars of the Book of Joshua, explained to the class: "That was before God became a Christian"! For many Christians today, ministers and laity alike, the Bible is the New Testament for all practical purposes, with perhaps a few excursions into favorite passages such as the Twenty-third Psalm.

From time to time theologians of the church have advocated discarding the Old Testament from the Christian canon. One such scholar was the church historian Adolph Harnack (1851–1930). He became interested in a second-century Christian named Marcion, a follower of Paul who was expelled from the church at Rome (about 144 C.E.) because of his radical teachings, in particular his view that the Redeemer revealed in Jesus Christ is not the same God as the Creator-God of the Old Testament. In his monumental work *Marcion: The Gospel of the Strange God*, Harnack stated that in the second century the church properly refused to reject the Old Testament, *that* in the sixteenth century the retention of the Old Testament was a fateful necessity *that* the Reformation was not yet able to escape, but *that* in the enlightened period since the nineteenth century the attempt to perpetuate the Old Testament in the Christian canon displays "a religious and ecclesiastical paralysis."[1]

This negative view of the Scriptures of Israel contrasts with the positive attitude of the early Christian community. The only Bible those early Christians had was the one shared in common with the Jewish community, sometimes referred to as the Torah (Law) and the Prophets. When Jesus said, according to the Gospel of Matthew (5:17), that he had not come to destroy but to fulfill the Torah and the Prophets, he was referring to this common bible. Indeed, whenever the word "scripture/s" (*graphe, graphai*) appears in the New Testament, the reference is almost always to the Jewish Bible, though usually in the form of the Greek translation (Septuagint) made in Alexandria, Egypt. Christians searched these Scriptures diligently, finding in them clues to the identity of Jesus and the purpose of God in history.

This is illustrated in the beautiful story, found in Luke 24, about the walk of two disciples from Jerusalem to the nearby village of Emmaus. It was a time of sadness, after Jesus' execution by crucifixion and before the news of Jesus' resurrection had spread. As the two walked in the lengthening shadow of the cross, so the story goes, Jesus joined them incognito. The stranger proceeded to explain to them on the basis of Scripture (that is, the Torah of Moses, the Prophets, and the Psalms) that Jesus' suffering, death, and victory actually occurred in the context of God's purpose. And later, according to the story, they exclaimed, "Were not our hearts burning within us . . . while he was opening the Scriptures to us?" (Luke 24:32).

This incident shows that early Christian evangelists did not advocate going beyond or rejecting the Scriptures of Israel, but rather, they advocated rereading the common Bible shared by Jews and Christians. In due time

Christians produced their own Scriptures, which were called the New Testament (Covenant), and joined these writings with the received Scriptures, which they called the Old Testament (Covenant). The apocalyptic titles for these two volumes of the Christian Bible were derived from Jeremiah's prophecy that the age of the old covenant ultimately would be superseded by a new age, the age of the new covenant (Jer. 31:31–34). The point is that Christians, like the community of the new covenant at Qumran, engaged in a creative rereading of the Jewish Bible. Sacred tradition was reinterpreted in the light of new experience or, as Christians perceived, a new revelation of God in the words and deeds of Jesus of Nazareth.

The Storytelling Manner of Confessing Faith

The way to begin discussing the relation between the Old and New Testaments is not to start with two bodies of literature, set over against each other, but with a common Bible, differently interpreted in two communities of faith, the Jewish and the Christian, synagogue and church. These communities have something else in common: they confess their faith characteristically by telling a story or reciting a history.

Back in 1941, H. Richard Niebuhr, professor of theology at Yale Divinity School, published an important book called *The Meaning of Revelation*. It has become a modern religious classic. In the second chapter, entitled "The Story of Our Life," he argued that a historical approach is indispensable in the Christian community precisely because the gospel itself finds expression in the telling of a story or a history. He wrote that the early Christian community apparently

> felt that to speak in confessional terms about the events that had happened to it in its history was not a burdensome necessity but rather an advantage and that the

acceptance of an historical point of view was not confining but liberating. The preaching of the early Christian church was not an argument for the existence of God nor an admonition to follow the dictates of some common human conscience, unhistorical or super-historical in character. It was primarily a simple recital of the great events connected with the historical appearance of Jesus Christ and a confession of what had happened to the community of disciples.[2]

Even today Christians confess their faith by telling or singing about "the old, old story."

It is interesting that Niebuhr, as though anticipating the storytelling theology that has become influential in our time,[3] preferred the word *story*, at least in the title of this chapter, though he alternated it with the word *history*. Since the appearance of his book almost forty years ago, a lot of theological water has gone under the bridge and, as someone has quipped, a lot of theological bridges have gone under the water. One of the big problems has been the word *history*, and particularly God's presence and action in history.

According to Webster's New World Dictionary (Second College Edition), "story" is defined as a series of connected events, true or fictitious, that is written or told with the intention of entertaining or informing. It says further that the ancestry of this word goes back through Middle English *storie* to Old French *estoire* to Latin *historia*, and we are also advised: "See History." There is a very fine line between story and history; in fact, in some languages one word covers both, as in German *Geschichte*. The biblical story is not history, if you mean a detached spectator's report of events; and the biblical history is not story, if you mean a tale spun out of the pure imagination of a storyteller. What we are talking about is a historylike story or a storylike history. That is what Niebuhr had in mind, I believe, when he said that Christians confess their faith by telling and retelling a story. Indeed, our English word *gospel* goes back to the Middle English *godspel,* which meant "good story" and by a change of inflection, "God-story."

Early Christians, however, did not invent this storytelling theology. They were profoundly influenced by the Jewish community, which likewise confessed its faith in terms of a story/history. In his chapter "The Story of Our Life," Niebuhr recognizes this. When early Christian preachers expressed their faith by telling the story of their life, he wrote:

> They followed in this respect the prophets who had spoken of God before them and the Jewish community which had also talked of revelation. These, too, always spoke of history, of what happened to Abraham, Isaac, and Jacob [and we may add, to Sarah, and Rebekah, Rachel, and Leah], of a deliverance from Egypt, of the covenant of Sinai, of mighty acts of God.[4]

This kind of *godspel,* or gospel, the early Christian community inherited from the people Israel to whom they are united—as Paul put it metaphorically in his important discussion in Romans 9–11—as a wild olive shoot is grafted into an olive tree (Rom. 11:17–24). Jews and Christians stand on the same ground insofar as they have a storytelling faith.

The Narrative Character of Israel's Faith

Let us look, then, at the Hebrew Bible—the Scriptures that the Christian community received as sacred tradition. This library of books is characterized by great diversity—different literary types, styles of expression, theological views. Yet in the midst of its great diversity, one thing stands out clearly, and that is the narrative character of Israel's faith. The faith of this community finds expression in the telling of a story.

The great Jewish novelist Elie Wiesel begins one of his novels, *The Gates of the Forest,* by telling a parable:

When the great Rabbi Israel Baal Shem-Tov saw misfortune threatening the Jews, it was his custom to go into a certain part of the forest to meditate. There he would light a fire, say a special prayer, and the miracle would be accomplished and the misfortune averted.

Later, when his disciple, the celebrated Magid of Mezritch, had occasion, for the same reason, to intercede with Heaven, he would go to the same place in the forest and say: "Master of the Universe, listen! I do not know how to light the fire, but I am still able to say the prayer." And again the miracle would be accomplished.

Still later, Rabbi Moshe-Leib of Sasov, in order to save his people once more, would go into the forest and say: "I do not know how to light the fire, I do not know the prayer, but I know the place and this must be sufficient." It was sufficient and the miracle was accomplished.

Then it fell to Rabbi Israel of Rishyn to overcome misfortune. Sitting in his armchair, his head in his hands, he spoke to God: "I am unable to light the fire, and I do not know the prayer; I cannot even find the place in the forest. All I can do is to tell the story, and this must be sufficient." And it was sufficient.

God made [human beings] because God loves stories.[5]

This parable provides a good introduction to the Jewish Bible. The Bible is full of stories: the story of creation, the story of the great flood, the story of deliverance from Egypt, the story of David's rise to be king of Israel, the story of Ruth and Naomi—all sorts of stories. Storytelling is essential to the faith of this community and has been from the very first.

Moreover, when you look at the Bible as a whole, it is one unfolding story. This is especially evident when one turns to the Torah, or Pentateuch (Genesis through Deuteronomy)—the basic and most authoritative part of the Hebrew Bible in Jewish tradition. Indeed, the Hebrew term *torah* is inadequately rendered as "law" (NT: *nomos*); the Jewish translation, *Tanakh*, properly renders the term as "teaching." The Torah includes laws, but fundamentally it is teaching in the form of a story that begins with creation and moves toward the horizon of God's purpose.

Here again, as in the New Testament, we face the problem of story versus history. For centuries people believed that the Bible presents a reliable account of ancient history, including such events as the expulsion from the garden of Eden, the great flood, the migration of Abraham from Ur of Babylonia, Joseph's administration of Egypt, and so forth. In those earlier centuries, before the Enlightenment of the eighteenth and nineteenth centuries, people could not go to libraries of universities and read books on the history of civilization or the history of Israel. Lacking the critical histories that are available to us, the biblical record was taken to be straightforward history. However, it has become increasingly apparent that the biblical account has the ambiguity of the German term *Geschichte*, which, as we have noted, may mean "history" or "story." At points, the account reflects crucial historical experiences, such as the exodus from Egypt, the Israelite settlement in Palestine, the rise of David as king of united Israel, the split of the Davidic kingdom into north and south, and the final fall of the north to the Assyrians in 722 B.C.E. and the south to the Babylonians in 587 B.C.E. Insofar as these events are historical, the record is open to historical-critical investigation and may be corroborated or challenged by the study of ancient history and by archaeology. Various attempts have been made to write a critical "history of Israel," the most recent being the one edited by Hershel Shanks.[6]

But the biblical account goes beyond "history" in the strict sense of the word into the realm of storytelling and poetry. The biblical narrative is a mixture of what we would distinguish as history and story. It is, as said previously, a historylike story or a storylike history, and it is often impossible to distinguish sharply between these two dimensions. Above all, it must be emphasized that the Bible was not written to chronicle ancient history. This is confessional literature, written to confess faith in the holy God, who gets involved in the life of a small people and, through the history of that people, claims to be recognized as Creator and Redeemer by all peoples. Like the writings of the New Testament, Israel's Scripture also is *godspel*, that is, good story, or God-story.

The Heart of the Story

The Bible, then, is Scripture shared by two communities, the Jewish and Christian, who have a story to tell. Their faith is not best expressed in propositions such as "I believe that God exists" or in eternal ideas such as "the good, the true, and the beautiful"; rather, their faith is characteristically expressed in narrative terms. God is the God of Abraham, Isaac, and Jacob (and the stories told about the ancestors); God is the God who spoke by prophets in concrete situations of life; God is the God who acted through Jesus of Nazareth. God speaks to us through human imagination, which creates and responds to stories, particularly the story that unfolds in the Bible.

These two communities differ, however, in the telling of the story and especially in their perception of the climactic moments of the story. For the Jewish community, the heart of the Bible is found in the Mosaic story—what we call the Torah, or the teaching that God gives the people in their historical pilgrimage as they appropriate their sacred heritage. For the Christian community, the heart and climax of the story is the Jesus story—the "good news" (gospel) announced by the four "gospel makers" who found anticipations of that great historical climax as they reread the Scriptures of Israel.

Let us consider for a moment the Torah—the so-called five books of Moses (Genesis through Deuteronomy). As said previously, this Torah is not "law" in the restrictive sense, though many commandments are included; rather, it is a great story, an extended narrative. Like a symphony, to use a musical figure, the Torah has several movements: the primeval history, the ancestral history, the exodus story, the Sinai story, the story of the wanderings in the wilderness, the story of the entry into the promised land. Each of these stories has its special character, but all of them belong to the great whole, the Torah story. When the Torah ends in the last chapter of the Book of Deuteronomy, with the death of Moses, the story is not over; for the people of God are summoned to go forward, the horizon of God's future beckons, God's promise is still on the way to fulfillment. The story is "to be continued."

Now, the heart of this story, according to Jewish reading, is found in the crucial experiences related in the Book of Exodus: the deliverance from Egyptian bondage and the sojourn at Mount Sinai, where a covenant was made between God and people. The whole Torah is issued under the aegis of Moses because he was the one who stood in the midst of these events as God's spokesperson; he was the originator of the whole tradition that centers in the experiences of Exodus and Sinai. This was the decisive period in the story of God's people. Later on, in a time of great crisis, when a dictator was on the throne and prophets were driven underground, Elijah made a pilgrimage back to Sinai, the Mosaic source of the tradition (1 Kings 19). That is the narrator's way of saying that the prophets also hark back to these seminal experiences of Exodus and Sinai. It is worth noting that in the story of Jesus' transfiguration (Mark 9:2–8 and parallels) both Moses and Elijah, the representatives of the Torah and the Prophets, appeared with Jesus on the mountain.

The Mosaic story, which narrates the Exodus and the sojourn at Mount Sinai, is surely a *godspel*, a good story, a God-story. The narrator develops the plot with dramatic effect as we are drawn into the contest between Pharaoh, the mightiest emperor of the day, and the God to whom slaves cried out for deliverance. But this is not mere fiction; the story is based upon the real experience of the liberating presence of God at the sea, when the fugitive Israelites sensed the miraculous presence of God, and Miriam and her companions led the people in singing and dancing. This happened, we believe, during the reign of Pharaoh Ramses II (1290–1224 B.C.E.), one of the great rulers of the Nineteenth Dynasty of ancient Egypt. The question is, What did the women perceive so that they broke out into ecstatic song? What prompted them to lead the community in "the dance of the merrymakers" (to use a phrase from Jer. 31:4)?

This question is treated beautifully and profoundly by Emil Fackenheim, a professor emeritus of philosophy at the University of Toronto, in his little book *God's Presence in History: Jewish Affirmations and Philosophical Reflections.* He starts with a Jewish midrash (commentary) based on the first verse of the Book of Ezekiel: "The heavens were opened, and I saw visions of God" (Ezek. 1:1). The Midrash affirms that what all Israel saw on earth, thanks to the perception of the women, was far more significant than what Ezekiel saw in heaven. He writes:

> The cited Midrash has special significance, however, because it affirms God's presence in history in full awareness of the fact that the affirmation is strange, extraordinary, or even paradoxical. The God of Israel . . . is so infinitely beyond human reach that an opening of the heavens themselves is required if [God] is to become humanly accessible. Few are [those] to whom such an opening was ever granted. . . . So infinitely is the Divine above the human! Nevertheless, the Midrash insists that not messengers, not angels, not intermediaries, but God Himself acts in human history—and [God] was unmistakably present to a whole people at least once.[7]

These twin experiences of salvation and obligation, of liberation and responsibility, Fackenheim terms "the saving experience" and "the commanding experience." Exodus deliverance and its corollary, Sinai obedience, are the "root experiences" of all Jewish tradition. These are the "seminal experiences" out of which the whole Torah has developed. Many generations have participated in the telling and retelling of the Torah story. At first it was preserved in song and story; later it was recorded in epic literature; eventually it was given canonical shape in the Torah we have received. But in the beginning was the story—the story of a marvelous experience of divine power breaking into this world to liberate slaves and make them a responsible people. For the people this was not history that slips into the past and becomes ancient; it was a story that was told and retold with contemporary meaning as "our story," the story of our life. Even today the Passover haggadah, or homily, reminds worshipers that "in every generation you must look upon yourself as if you personally had come forth from Egypt. . . . For it was not alone our ancestors whom the Holy One, Blessed be He, redeemed, but also us whom he redeemed with them." And today liberation theologians of the Third World find that this old, old story is filled with saving power.[8]

The Christian Story

The early Christians, as we have seen, shared this storytelling tradition. They believed that the Jesus story was part of the larger story that was unfolding from the creation on, as set forth in the Scriptures of Israel. The Bible that they read, that is, the Torah and the Prophets, did not belong to somebody else—only to the Jewish community; it belonged to them too. It was also the story of their life. They could say, as did the apostle Paul, that "these things were written down to instruct us, on whom the ends of the ages have come" (1 Cor. 10:11). Or as Paul puts it succinctly toward the conclusion of his epistle to the Romans: "Whatever was written in former days was written for our instruction, so that by steadfastness and by the encouragement of the scriptures we might have hope" (Rom. 15:4). In the Christian Communion service, worshipers join in praising and thanking God "for the goodness and love which you have made known to us in creation, in the calling of Israel to be your people, in your

Word spoken through the prophets, and above all in the Word made flesh, Jesus your Son." Creation, Israel, the prophets, Jesus Christ—that is the sequence of the great story that unfolds in the perspective of Christian faith.

There are, however, both agreements and differences between Jews and Christians in the reading and interpretation of the biblical story. I used to have luncheon discussions with my good friend and former colleague, Will Herberg, a Jewish philosopher who spent his climactic years teaching at Drew University. We spent much time talking about the affinities and differences between the Jewish and the Christian communities. He once wrote a fine essay in which he compared the Jewish Passover with Christian Easter.[9] The Passover service has profoundly influenced the Last Supper that Christians observe; indeed, the eucharistic words "the blood of the new covenant" echo the covenant service at the base of Mount Sinai where, in a sacramental blood rite, Moses said: "See the blood of the covenant that the LORD has made with you in accordance with all these words" (Exod. 24:8).

Yes, there is profound affinity between the Jewish and Christian communities, and thus there is continuity between the Testaments, Old and New. But there is also deep discontinuity, profound rupture. And that discontinuity, that rupture, is greatest and deepest at the cross, the experience that Christians remember and relive in their Sacrament of the Lord's Supper, or Eucharist. The experience of the cross, and its corollary, the presence of God in human history—a divine breaking into history with saving power and imperative obligation—is comparable to Exodus and Sinai in some respects. Jews and Christians do stand together on the conviction of the presence of God in human history. Not in some realm above history, not in some quiet place of the human heart, but here in the concreteness of human history, where people are suffering and crying out for deliverance from bondage, God is present. However, it is the preaching of Jesus Christ crucified that is the fundamental stumbling block to the Jewish community, even as it is foolishness to the philosophers of the Gentile world (1 Cor. 1:18–31).

The plain truth is that, short of conversion, there is no clear path that leads from the Scriptures of Israel to the gospel of the early Christian church. The Old Testament (Hebrew Bible) does not necessarily lead to the New: it could, and did, lead to the Talmud and continuing rabbinical tradition; or it could lead to the Koran and to the religion of radical monotheism. To quote the final lines of my *Understanding the Old Testament*, which have remained essentially unchanged in all four editions: "The scriptures of Israel end like an incomplete drama. According to Pharisaic Judaism, Israel's pilgrimage leads through the Hebrew Bible to the Talmud and a continued life of messianic expectancy. According to the early Christian community, the pilgrimage of the people of God leads through the Old Testament to Jesus Christ, who came not to destroy but to fulfill the Torah and the Prophets."[10]

We must take seriously the open-endedness of the Old Testament. So much depends on the answer that one gives to the question of the identity of Jesus of Nazareth. The turning point in the story of Jesus, as we read it in the Gospel of Mark, is an incident that occurred in the region of Caesarea-Philippi. There Jesus put the question to his disciples: "Who do people say that I am?" (8:27). The answer was something like this: "Some say this, some say that; maybe you're one of the prophets, like Jeremiah; maybe a wonder-worker, like Hellenistic magicians." But Jesus pressed the question: "But who do you say that I am?" (8:29). Peter responded, speaking for the community of believers: "You are the Messiah" (8:29). That is not an easy answer, as evident from Peter's immediate misunderstanding about the path of suffering that Jesus must tread. But when the answer to "the christological question" is given in faith—and, I repeat, it cannot be given easily—that answer changes one's whole perspective. Then with eyes of faith one may reread the Scriptures of Israel and perceive that the story of Jesus is part of "the great story and plot of all time and space," as Amos Wilder puts it.[11] Indeed, seen in the perspective of Christian faith, the whole biblical story, which extends from creation to consummation, reaches its climax in the life, death, and resurrection of Jesus Christ and the new age in human history that he introduced.

The Coexistence of Synagogue and Church

The confession of faith that Jesus is the Christ raises inescapably the question with which we began and which has been lurking at our footsteps all along the way—the coexistence of synagogue and church. These two communities of faith belong to one people who share the same Scriptures and yet differ over "the christological question," that is, the identity of Jesus of Nazareth. Christians and Jews have a lot to talk about, and there are many evidences of ongoing conversation, such as the book by Professor Fritz Rothschild of Jewish Theological Seminary entitled *Jewish Perspectives on Christianity: The Views of Five Twentieth-Century Thinkers.*[12] In this discussion I have proposed that the question of the relation between the Testaments (a Christian formulation) reaches out into a larger and more basic question, the relation between the Jewish and Christian communities.

In the Christian community we oversimplify—if not escape—the question when we engage in Christianizing of the Old Testament. This is sometimes done by Christian interpreters who enthusiastically seize the Scriptures of Israel with such passion that these writings are made to bear witness not just to Christ, but to Jesus Christ. An illustration of this Christian enthusiasm is Wilhelm Vischer's *The Witness of the Old Testament to Christ,* in which, for instance, Jacob's nocturnal wrestle with a stranger at the ford of the Jabbok River (Gen. 32:22–32) is construed to portray an encounter with the Lord Jesus Christ.[13] A more excellent way has been proposed by Dietrich Bonhoeffer, the Christian theologian who was martyred during the Nazi period. In his advocacy of theological maturity, or Christianity that "has come of age," Bonhoeffer turned away from christological exposition of the Old Testament, as he had done in his *Creation and Fall*, and proposed that Christian readers turn directly to the Old Testament. In an Advent meditation, composed during his final days in prison, he spoke about how his thoughts and feelings were more and more influenced by the Old Testament. "It is only when one knows the ineffability of the Name of God," he wrote, "that one can utter the name of Jesus Christ. It is only when one loves life and the world so much that without them everything would be gone, that one can believe in the resurrection and a new life." He goes on to say, "I don't think it is Christian to want to get to the New Testament too soon and too directly."[14]

I was once called upon to respond to a paper by Matitiahu Tsevat on "Theology of the Old Testament: A Jewish View." He admitted the novelty of his presentation, for in Jewish circles "Old Testament Theology," he said, is almost unheard of—something like "the zoology of a unicorn." His thesis was that the Old Testament should be allowed to speak for itself, independently, rather than being ancillary to the Talmud. At one point he used a marvelous illustration—the airport passenger conveyor belt that connects both ends of a long passageway. It is easy enough to take it in one direction, he said, for "the Talmud understands itself to be a continuation and supplement of the Old Testament."[15] But if one wants to reverse the direction, and move from the Talmud to the Old Testament, the effort demands incredible exertion. It is well nigh impossible.

I can agree that similar exertion is demanded if Christians are to allow the Hebrew Bible, which they call the Old Testament, to make its own theocentric witness. In part, this theological exertion involves coming to terms with the coexistence of the Jewish and Christian communities in the purpose of God.

That issue Paul grapples with in his agonized discussion in Romans 9–11, where he considers God's faithfulness to the promises made to Israel and how, in the face of the rejection of Jesus Christ, Israel can be saved. A mighty struggle goes on in these chapters, and I can touch on it only briefly. In his book *The Origins of Anti-Semitism* (1983), John Gager maintains that in the view of Romans 9–11 Jesus was not the climax of the story of God's dealings with Israel, and therefore the salvation of Israel does not lie in turning to Christianity.[16] For the Jews, according to Gager, salvation is by way of the Torah; for Gentiles, salvation comes through Jesus Christ. Now it is quite true that Paul's discussion provides no basis for anti-Semitism; however, the proposed solution is all too simple, for it does not do justice to Paul's anguish over his kinfolk, or to his conviction about the centrality of Jesus Christ in God's ecumenical purpose. It is far better to recognize, to use Paul's own language, that the coexistence of these two communities of faith, Jewish and Christian, and the eschatological realization of the promise that "all Israel will be saved" comprise a mystery hidden in the sovereign purpose and elective grace of God. It is that mystery that prompts the apostle to exclaim at the conclusion of his anguished and not altogether logical discussion: "O the depth of the riches and wisdom and knowledge of God! How unsearchable are [God's] judgments and how inscrutable [God's] ways!" (Rom. 11:33).

That is the mystery, I believe, to which the discussion of the relation between the Testaments belongs. The Jewish and Christian communities belong together as closely as twins in the womb of God's creative purpose. In a profound sense, both communities belong to Israel, the people of God. They have in common a Bible that is the shared history of this one people. They differ—and probably will differ until the *eschaton* (the end of history)—over the question of the climax of the story. The moot question is whether the pilgrimage of God's people leads through the Hebrew Bible to the Talmud and a continued life of messianic expectancy, or whether that pilgrimage leads through the Old Testament to Jesus, the Christ, who came not to destroy but to fulfill the Torah and the Prophets.

Notes

1. Cited in the Introduction to the symposium I edited, *The Old Testament and Christian Faith* (New York, Evanston, and London: Harper & Row, Publishers, 1963), 5.

2. H. Richard Niebuhr, *The Meaning of Revelation* (New York: Macmillan, 1941), 43.

3. See, e.g., Gabriel Fackre, *The Christian Story: A Narrative Interpretation of Basic Christian Doctrine*, vol. 1 (Grand Rapids: Wm. B. Eerdmans, 1978).

4. Niebuhr, *The Meaning of Revelation*, 45–46.

5. Elie Wiesel, *The Gates of the Forest* trans. Frances Frenaye (New York: Schocken Books, 1982); orig. pub. New York: Holt, Rinehart, and Winston, 1966.

6. Hershel Shanks, ed., *Ancient Israel* (Englewood Cliffs, N.J.: Prentice-Hall, 1988).

7. Emil Fackenheim, *God's Presence in History: Jewish Affirmations and Philosophical Reflections* (New York: Harper Torchbooks, 1978), 4.

8. See, e.g., Jose Severino Croatto, *Exodus: A Hermeneutics of Freedom*, trans. Salvator Atanasio (Maryknoll, N.Y.: Orbis Books, 1981).

9. Will Herberg, "Beyond Time and Eternity: Reflections on Passover and Easter," in *Faith Enacted as History*, ed. Bernhard W. Anderson (Philadelphia: Westminster Press, 1976), 67–71.

10. Bernhard W. Anderson, *Understanding the Old Testament* (Englewood Cliffs, N.J.: Prentice-Hall, 1957; 4th ed., 1986), 643.

11. Amos Wilder, *The Language of the Gospel* (New York: Harper & Row, 1964), 64.

12. Fritz Rothschild, ed., *Jewish Perspectives on Christianity: The Views of Five Twentieth-Century Thinkers* (New York: Cross-

road, 1990). Selections from the writings of Leo Beck, Martin Buber, Franz Rosensweig, Will Herberg, and Abraham Heschel are each introduced by a Christian theologian.

13. Wilhelm Vischer, *The Witness of the Old Testament to Christ* (London: Lutterworth Press, trans., A.B. Crabtree 1948), 153–54.

14. The reference to *Creation and Fall* is quoted from *Prisoner for God: Letters and Papers from Prison*, trans. Reginald H. Fuller (New York: The MacMillan Co., 1960), 32–33. Cf. Dietrich Bonhoeffer, *Creation and Fall (A Theological Interpretation of Genesis 1–3* (New York: MacMillan, 1959).

15. Matitiahu Tsevat, "Theology of the Old Testament: A Jewish View," in *Horizons in Biblical Theology*, ed. Ulrich Mauser (8: June, 1986), 33–59.

16. John Gager, *The Origins of Anti-Semitism:* Attitudes toward Judaism in Pagan and Christian Antiquity (New York: Oxford University Press, 1983). 197–264, esp. 223–25.

2

What Has the Old Testament to Do with the New?

James H. Charlesworth

Why should Christians continue to read the Old Testament? Is it not supplanted by the New Testament? When there is so little time for most Christians to read, should they not read only what is essential, and is that not the New Testament writings, and perhaps only Paul's Romans and the Gospel According to John? With our wise appreciation of the new and the advances of our time, should we not focus on one main question: "What is new?" Is that not the way we often address old friends? And so, is it not prudent for us to celebrate and honor the New Testament within the Bible? Are not our publishers right to give us at times only the New Testament or the New Testament with Psalms?

What is the relevance of the Old Testament for the New Testament? What is the relation of the Testaments? Throughout the world Christians would tend to agree that the Old Testament writings, especially the prophetic books, pointed to the coming of the Messiah of Israel, and that Jesus was indeed this Messiah awaited by all Jews. Are not great sermons based on the proclamation that Jesus is the fulfillment of messianic prophecies?

Why ask, therefore, "What is the relation of the Testaments?" Is not the appropriate answer something like the following: Jesus is the Christ promised by God;

indeed, the Old Testament contains the promises and the New Testament explains the fulfillment.

These are clear answers. And the New Testament works themselves could be mined to prove the accuracy of the conclusion. The author of Luke-Acts, for example, has Jesus' ministry begin in the Nazareth synagogue. Jesus stands up and reads from Isaiah 61, and then states, "Today this scripture has been fulfilled in your hearing" (Luke 4:21). Earlier, when Jesus, as a baby, was presented to the priests in the Temple, Simeon—who was promised by the Holy Spirit that he would not die until he had seen "the Lord's Christ"—looks on Jesus, holds him in his arms, and blesses God with the words "my eyes have seen your salvation" (Luke 2:30). Likewise, Paul begins his major work, Romans, with the claim that Jesus Christ is God's good news, which God "promised beforehand through his prophets in the holy scriptures" (Rom. 1:2). The usual emphasis in the New Testament writings is that the relation between the Old and New Testaments is one of promise and fulfillment.

Promise and Fulfillment

The promise-fulfillment approach to the relation of the Testaments has much to commend it. Christians ultimately would admit that in some ways Jesus fulfills God's promises. Through him Christians have continuously experienced the presence of the God made known in the "Old Testament" Scriptures. In some sense Jesus, for us Christians, is the "One-who-was-to-come." We are not looking for another; we are not searching the Old Testament promises to predict the advent of someone unknown.

The promise-fulfillment model, however, should not be pushed as the only way to view the relation of the Testaments. Nor should it be employed mechanically, as if Isaiah or another prophet predicted the birth, crucifixion, and resurrection of Jesus of Nazareth.[1] The method should be used with an appreciation of the original historical setting of individuals such as the prophets and the evangelists.

Two separate ways of perceiving the relation of the Testaments need to be joined. The *historical* and *retrospective* perspectives should not be defined as opposing (antithetical) categories. It is important for Christians to see the historical and social origins of the writings in the Bible. Also, they know that the appearance of Christ in history is conceivable because of expectations and traditions that predate Jesus of Nazareth by hundreds of years; hence, a glance backward is essential in a confession like "God . . . [sent] the Son into the world" (John 3:17).

The *historical* perspective does lead to an appreciation of a relationship. The Testaments are not chronologically separate but phenomenologically related in the sense that Paul, the evangelists, and most of the New Testament authors were part of, or were related to, the history of Judaism. The New Testament is not a late product of the church; most of it is a part of the literature of pre-Mishnaic Judaism.

The *retrospective* perspective is not merely subjective; it is grounded in the historical confessions that relate, for example, Second Isaiah to First Isaiah, and Peter's speeches (according to the author of Acts) to the Psalter, Isaiah, and other Scriptures. As Walther Zimmerli stated long ago, by the time of the Yahwist in the tenth century B.C.E. "the entire patriarchal history appears under the sign of promise." The promise is "nothing rigid or crystallized"; it developed through processes of "turbulent elaboration" so that the credo, the Deuteronomist, and other sections of the Old Testament are shaped by the promise-fulfillment category.[2]

The category, therefore, does not appear unexpectedly in the New Testament; it flows from significant dimensions of the Old Testament. The promises popping up intermittently throughout Genesis are frequently described as at least partially fulfilled in the narratives that follow in Exodus and elsewhere.

The Christian's task in perceiving the relation of the Testaments, consequently, is stretched from the development of the credo in the Old Testament to the goals of hermeneutics today. It is also a task that is not merely a parochial concern of the confessing Christian in a pluralistic world; it encompasses four thousand years (and more) of history and of diverse cultures in which promises were lived out, expected, and at times affirmed as fulfilled. The process entailed hundreds of years of interpretation and reinterpretation. The Christian affirms that the God of Jesus is identical with the one who had disclosed himself earlier: "I am the LORD who brought you from Ur of the Chaldeans, to give you this land to possess" (Gen. 15:7).

Christians need to retain, in a form shaped by their own understandings, the promise-fulfillment paradigm. Otherwise, they would forfeit the desired link celebrated with the New Testament authors. Obviously, Christians need to guard against claiming either that the Old flows directly into the New or affirming the outmoded assumption that Isaiah actually saw Christ—as the author of the Ascension of Isaiah claimed[3]—without jettisoning the New Testament proclamations that Jesus fulfills God's promises.[4]

The promise-fulfillment explanation of the relation of the Testaments should not distort the Christian bible or misrepresent the attractively rich complexities of early Christianity. In the past, the advocates of this model did not adequately confront some of the major questions. Were Jews looking for the coming of the Messiah? If they were, why is there so little evidence for this belief in the Old Testament Apocrypha and Pseudepigrapha, the Dead Sea Scrolls, and Philo? Why did Jesus, according to extant sources, never mention or discuss God's Messiah? Why are his disciples never portrayed asking him about the

Messiah? Why does Mark, in the judgment of most scholars the earliest Gospel, not portray Jesus as accepting and
approving of Peter's confession that he is the Christ (the
Greek translation of the Hebrew word *Messiah*)?

The promise-fulfillment model for answering the
question of the relation of the Testaments helps us grasp
the continuity and the dynamic enthusiasm of Jesus' early
followers, but it tends to perpetuate a selective reading of
the Scriptures. It does not adequately represent the diversity either in the Old Testament or in the New Testament,
or the complexities and richness of the relationship.

To portray the Old Testament only as promise does not
account for the fulfillment recorded in it. God made three
promises to Abraham: he would have a special relation to
the Creator; he would inherit "the promised land" of Palestine; and he would be the father of many people. The
first promise was fulfilled at Sinai, with the giving of the
Ten Commandments and the clarification of God's will
(Torah). The second promise was fulfilled under Joshua
and finally David. The third promise was fulfilled through
the centuries; the wandering band of twelve tribes became
a majestic nation significant in international diplomacy.[5]

To depict the New Testament only as "fulfillment"
fails to appreciate that its authors sometimes point to
events not yet completed. Jesus' entire mission is characterized by the claim that God's rule—the kingdom of
God—was beginning to dawn in history. He pointed to
the future for its consummation. The author of Luke-Acts
describes the ascension of Jesus, and a promise is given
to the disciples that Jesus would return again in the same
way that he was taken from them (Acts 1:11). This promise shaped much of Paul's thought; in 1 Thessalonians
4:16 he describes how Jesus will return on the clouds and
in glory. The author of Revelation concludes his book
with the prayer "Come, Lord Jesus!" (Rev. 22:20). And
this yearning expectation for Jesus' return probably provides the meaning of the early Christian prayer *Marana
tha*, "Our Lord, come!" (1 Cor. 16:22; see Didache 10:6).

The promise-fulfillment explanation of the relation of the Testaments, indeed no one solution, can do justice to the complexities and diversities in both the Old and New Testaments. These ancient canons are a library of books. They were written by diverse peoples, in different times, and in various places. What then can be the relation between the books in the Old Testament and the books in the New Testament?

This issue was once a storm center of biblical research. In the fifties and sixties numerous books were focused on this major theme. Prestigious and revered Old Testament specialists wrote books on Old Testament theology, and they often concluded with a pinpointed discussion of the relation of the Old Testament to the New Testament.

Walther Eichrodt

Walther Eichrodt saw the center of the Old Testament to be the covenant made between God and Israel. "Covenant" for this German scholar denoted that God is grasped not speculatively but in concrete events in history. God's will is discernible so that an "atmosphere of trust and security" is created. Allegiance to Yahweh alone brought Israel together with solidarity and with commonality. Israel confronted God in historical deeds, thereby receiving an "interior attitude to history." Israel's religion is protected from being the tool of a nationalistic state and from the errors of a pantheistic worship of nature by its election. These impressive insights both contribute to our understanding of the Old Testament and lay a basis for a careful exploration of the relation of the Testaments.

Eichrodt stressed the unity of the Testaments. He pointed to what he saw as process, growth, and development. The two Testaments are united, he argued, because both record the "irruption of the Kingship of God into this world and its establishment here."[6] History is linear and directed toward one definite paradisiacal end (teleology). Eichrodt concluded that the predictions of the prophets are fulfilled in the revelation of Christ.

In light of the developments that separate us today from Eichrodt and his time, it seems fair to state that we can no longer simply appropriate his solution. On the one hand, he had to distort or ignore major portions of the Old Testament, such as all the Wisdom books like Proverbs and Ecclesiastes. On the other hand, he tended to recast the New Testament books as if they were theological reflections on the concept of covenant. Many Semitic concepts slip through the cracks. Although no clear consensus has emerged,[7] many Old Testament specialists now conclude that Julius Wellhausen was correct to argue that covenant was not an aspect of the early religion of Israel.[8] Covenant theology does not represent the thought of Hosea in the eighth century B.C.E. and those before him.

Eichrodt's concept of covenant is too broad. For him covenant was a "living process."[9] He showed that "covenant" was not a static concept introduced at Sinai; it was passed on with renewed appreciation and creative interpretation. But if "covenant" is a "living process," are we not dangerously close to changing a principle that sustained solidarity with a fluctuating concept?

Eichrodt has helped us grasp how important is the concept of "covenant" in both Testaments and what a significant place it must play in seeking to discover the relation of the Testaments. We cannot, however, proceed as if either Testament can be reduced to deposits of theological reflections on the "covenant" or a record of the development of the concept. Yet covenant is a major factor in both Testaments, in the ways the New relates to the Old, and in the Judaism of Jesus' time.[10]

Gerhard von Rad

More successful was the attempt of the great German Old Testament theologian Gerhard von Rad. He rejected all attempts to reduce the complexities in the Old Testament to one or even a list of essential elements. He was impressed with the variety of theological thoughts in the Old Testament.

Von Rad showed that there are "tremendous differences" between the Old Testament literary strata. He argued that theologians must attempt to discern what Israel herself testified about Yahweh. Claiming that each writing must be studied in terms of its own proclamation (kerygmatic intention), he demonstrated that Israel's faith was grounded in a theology of history, and he stressed that God's divine acts in history are not the results of modern scientific investigations but the faith confessions in Israel. He illustrated that "faith" for Israel was neither an object to be discerned nor the "subject of Israel's confessional utterances." Hence, Israel had no theology or religion as an entity. The essence of the Old Testament theologies is the ". . . living word of Jahweh coming on and on to Israel for ever, and this in [sic] the message uttered by his mighty acts."[11]

Eichrodt and von Rad concluded that both Testaments record the confessions that God has appeared in history through God's saving acts (*Heilsgeschichte*). In contrasting ways, both scholars claimed that despite its heterogeneity, the Old Testament points to the Christ event of the New Testament. Both wisely emphasized that faith, in each Testament, is faith in a person—Yahweh or Christ. Each of these arguments continues to be significant in our search for the relation of the Testaments, but I would prefer concluding that the Old Testament prepares for (not points to) the Christ event of the New Testament.

Von Rad urged us to comprehend that Yahweh and Christ are described as grasped only partially and in terms of contrasts with known phenomena (*sub specie contraria*). God and Christ are perceived to be hidden and mysterious. For von Rad, the "whole history of the covenant is simply the history of God's continuous retreat."[12]

A major contribution by von Rad is his insight that the real link between the Testaments is the linguistic-conceptual chain. Jesus' earliest followers were "able to continue to use the language of the Old Testament, to link on to it, and to avail" themselves of "this linguistic tool."[13] This major point needs to be modified in light of the redefinition of terms and the appearance of new terms and concepts in the writings that bridge the chasm from the latest Old Testament writings to the New Testament documents.

Von Rad was impressed with the expectation quality of the Old Testament; from Abraham to Malachi, Israel was pregnant with expectation, yearning for "something yet to come."[14] Seeing that the Old Testament, especially the Hexateuch, is arranged beneath a "threefold arch of prophecy and fulfillment," von Rad stressed that the Old Testament must be read so that "expectation keeps mounting up to vast proportions."[15] Although the prophets were not clairvoyant and spoke only predictions that were "prefigurations,"[16] the Old Testament is to be interpreted as "pointing to the future fulfillment in Jesus Christ."

For von Rad, "the coming of Jesus Christ as a historical reality leaves the exegete no choice at all; he must interpret the Old Testament as pointing to Christ whom he must understand in its light."[17] When von Rad wrote "exegete" he probably meant Christian exegete; and that clarification reveals a problem acutely felt by those of us who are striving to develop a basis for Christian exegesis that is not exclusivistic, an exegesis that not only maintains the integrity of the Christian but is acceptable in a pluralistic society.[18] For me there is far more truth in von Rad's recognition that Christ must be understood in light of the Old Testament than in his claim that the Old Testament points to Christ.

Significantly, von Rad focused attention on the age-old concept of typology. For him there is a typological relation between the Testaments. He rightly warns

against seeing David, Joshua, the Tabernacle, or the Passover lamb as "types" of Christ.[19] For him typological
interpretation is possible if it goes beyond the historical
self-understandings of the Old Testament authors themselves. They are not themselves aware of what they are
the preparation for. At this point I must confess some
perplexity at what such claims have to do with the particularity, historicity, and contingency of the human utterances in our Scriptures. Are we dangerously close to
creating texts? In what ways do the attempts to move
beyond the Old Testament authors' self-understanding
lead us toward the Mishnah and the Talmudim and not
toward the New Testament? The Old Testament certainly
leads forward to each of these writings, and so our search
for the relation of the Testaments must not be so myopic
that it sees only two Testaments.

Von Rad has clearly seen the diversities in the theologies of the so-called Old Testament. He emphasized the
need to continue in a revised form a study of the typological relationship. Many of his comments, however, are
poetic and confessional, leaving the impression that he
has in places written as a historian and scholar and elsewhere as a preacher and prophet.

Rudolf Bultmann

The New Testament scholar who dedicated his life to
a study of the theologies in the New Testament, searched
for a unifying theme among the New Testament writings,
and published on the perplexing issue of the relation of
the Testaments was Rudolf Bultmann. More than that of
any other scholar, his position derives from his philosophical stance and presuppositions. Approaching the
New Testament and the relation of the Testaments with
the logic of existentialism, he urged us to consider what
the Old Testament has to say to our own situation and
our endeavors to understand the meaning of human

existence (*Daseinsverständnis*).[20] Our dialogue with the Old Testament should be to reveal to us the meaning of our own existence.

Bultmann saw the Old Testament only in terms of its promise, which meant for him how it prepared for the Christian understanding of existence. Tending to denigrate the significance of critical historical research and the search for the original setting and meaning of the Old Testament strata, Bultmann advised that we must prune the message from "its original reference to the Israelite people and their history."[21] He also claimed that the Old Testament is the word of God only if we "inviolably" hold that it be shorn of its historical setting and reference to the Israelite people and if only the promises are adopted. He argued that the Old Testament history is one of failure, especially of covenant and theocracy, and that the Old Testament receives its validity only from Christ.

Hearing such advice would lead many to conclude that Bultmann's advice is dangerous, distortionistic, and ideological. Bultmann, however, was certainly no Marcion, as Bernhard Anderson showed long ago;[22] he did not want to jettison the Old Testament from the canon, and he repudiated the idea that the Old Testament revealed an evil god.[23]

On hearing that the Old Testament must be freed from its connection with "the Israelite people" and obtains its validity only in Jesus Christ, some may conclude that Bultmann is simply anti-Semitic. This conclusion fails to observe that he stood against the Nazis,[24] presented a lecture in 1933 that denounced the treatment of Jews in Germany,[25] helped write the Marburg faculty's opposition to the Lutheran Church's regulation that all pastors support the state and be Aryan,[26] helped found the Confessing Church,[27] signed the Barmen Declaration of 1934,[28] lost a brother in one of Hitler's concentration camps, refused to alter his lectures as the Nazis desired, preached against the Nazis' nationalistic myths,[29] and supported the work of his student, the famous Jew Hans Jonas.[30]

Bultmann is one of the most difficult scholars to understand and is frequently misinterpreted. He was frustratingly contradictory and often made bold and blunt declarations that were occasionally supported by an earlier uncited publication or developed in some subsequent work. His penchant not to define terms carefully causes misunderstandings.[31] To a certain extent, the widespread misunderstanding of Bultmann can be traced to him and the turbulent times in which he lived.

The quotations from Bultmann in the previous paragraphs are not typical of his best thoughts. He did point out that the New Testament does not presuppose the *concrete* Old Testament. He also showed that the Old Testament cannot be united exclusively under the concept of law, because the Old Testament understanding of law is existence under grace.

Bultmann claimed that the New Testament does not simply repeat the proclamations of Jesus but first and foremost proclaims him. Christ is God's eschatological deed that brings to an end all ethnic history (*Volksgeschichte*). Christ is the end of salvation history (*Heilsgeschichte*) not because he is the goal of history but because he is its eschatological end. The message in Jesus Christ is the "Word" preached in and by the church. Hence, the Old Testament is necessary only because it is the preunderstanding (*Vorverständnis*) of the New. The presupposition is that we "must stand under the Old Testament . . . to understand the New."[32]

In a probing and critical essay on prophecy and fulfillment, Bultmann showed that the New Testament authors, in the attempt to prove the fulfillment of promise, read back into the Old Testament works their own beliefs, altered prophecies to suit the eisegesis, and were sometimes guilty of treating the Old Testament writings arbitrarily.[33] He admits that the traditional use of the promise-fulfillment paradigm "has become impossible," and recognizes that J. C. K. von Hofmann's two-volumed *Weissagung und Erfüllung* (*Prophecy and Fulfillment*) of 1841 and 1844 was a helpful attempt to see fulfillment not of Old Testament *words* but of Israel's *history.* Finally, this attempt is judged to be theologically irrelevant; it "naturally cannot provide a proof of the validity of Christ."[34] For Bultmann, von Hofmann's error was to assume the philosophical perspective that there is a process of development from the Old to the New. Bultmann replaces historical development with "eschatological end." Essentially, Bultmann advises us to give up the "naïve, traditional meaning of prophecy and fulfillment" and to accept the Pauline perspective whereby Christ is the end of the law (Rom. 10:4), the history of Israel is one of failure, and "Old Testament Jewish history" is fulfilled in the New Testament "in its contradiction, its miscarriage."[35]

Bultmann has made many suggestions that must be taken seriously, but they are not all on the same level. I can agree with him that we cannot continue to use the prophecy-fulfillment paradigm as had the authors of the New Testament, and that the Old Testament does not develop historically into the New Testament.

Bultmann has not adequately represented either the Old or the New Testament. The Old Testament history is not one of failure.[36] The authors of the New Testament did not offer that argument, and the appearance of the Mishnah, Tosephta, Talmudim, and Targumim are proofs that the Old Testament can be interpreted in appreciably other ways. The appeal to Paul does not take into account the complex ways Paul referred to the law and to Israel, and the evidence that he affirmed the continuing validity of God's covenantal promises to the Jews (Rom. 11:1).[37] Many passages in Romans indicate that Paul would have rejected Bultmann's claim that "God can reject the people he has chosen,"[38] that we must sever the promises from the land and the people of Israel, that Jews can be reproved as the "synagogue of Satan,"[39] and that the history of Israel led to its miscarriage. The appeal to eschatology serves too easily as a panacea. The claim that Christ is God's new beginning, a " 'new creation' in the eschatological sense"[40] demands a paradigm of discontinuities between Old and New Testaments and ignores that Jesus was a Jew, worshiped in the synagogues and Temple, sought to be faithful as a Jew to God's Scriptures and living word, and proclaimed the importance to Jews (and perhaps them alone) of the land and God's promises to his chosen ones, the Jews. Jesus' message was eschatological, but he grounded it in the history of his people and affirmed the inbreaking of God's rule (the kingdom of God) in his day and in the promised land.[41]

The significant contribution made by Bultmann is to try to retain the Christian Scriptures as a whole and as normative for a scientifically oriented person, who knows that the earth is not the center of the universe, that it does not revolve around the sun (which cannot stand still as the Old Testament claims), and that there is no abode of God and the angels in the heavens above the earth, and no hell, full of Satan and his hordes, cosmologically under the earth.

Bultmann's attempt to remove myth from the Scriptures (to demythologize them) failed because it misunderstood the mythic dimension of religious language, but it was a monumental attempt to create a new methodology and has helped give birth to methods more representative of the Bible and of our postmodern perceptions.[42]

Bultmann is complex. Certainly, he is not really interested in the Old Testament and Semitic culture. He attempts to understand everything from his own perspective and that of existentialism. Some of his positions seem contradictory; for example, how can he stress that the Old Testament must not be reduced to the concept of law and then conclude that the "material connection" between the Testaments is "between law and gospel," because the Old educates us toward faith by leading us into sin and boasting that we have been obedient and hence righteous before God?

Bultmann did not comprehend pre-70 Judaism and tended to perceive it from the misleading portrayals found in the New Testament. In this regard he was typical of his time.

Bultmann did not grasp the dimension of history in all human existence, and our time-bound search for understanding in light of our past. To focus only on present needs and our own existential situation betrays the historical dimensions of our life. We are linked with the past and can communicate with each other and ourselves (i.e., think) only because of our living relationship with and inheritance from our own private past and our culture's history.

The preceding rapid review of Eichrodt, von Rad, and Bultmann reveals that if we are accurately to comprehend the relations of the Testaments we must bring into view all of the Old Testament and all of the New Testament. We should also seek to discern the unique setting of each stratum of the traditions and not use modern definitions or be misled by twentieth-century philosophical systems. Our study of biblical theology should be cognizant of the vast advances in our understanding of archaeology and the history of "the Land," *Eretz* Israel. We should enable the truly otherness and offensiveness of different systems of thought and cultures to remain part of our inherited and cherished traditions. We dare not modernize and re-create texts that are divorced from traditions and historical events. Christianity is not an ideology or philosophy. It is a human response to God's revelation to real human beings and in actual geographical places.

Finally, and perhaps of most importance, our attempt to grasp the relation of the Testaments must not be in any way anti-Jewish or anti-Semitic. Today, fortunately, Jews are living in our communities and teaching alongside us. We dare not subjectively misrepresent the original meaning of the Hebrew Scriptures, or Old Testament. We should be able to defend our own positions from the charge of being unable to comprehend the original setting and language of prophets such as Isaiah and Jeremiah.

We should not slip into the tendency to suggest that the prophets pointed directly to Jesus as the Christ. We must not misread the Old Testament christologically. Its own integrity must be preserved if we really wish to learn what is the relation between it and the New.[43]

Three More Recent Attempts

Three scholars have struggled to rekindle the cooled debate over the relation of the Testaments. They are Brevard Childs, James Sanders, and Samuel Terrien. We can only scan their positions. In *Biblical Theology in Crisis* (Philadelphia: Westminster Press 1970), Childs claims that there is an unbroken continuity from the Old to the New Testaments. Beginning with the canon of the church, which has given us the Christian Bible, he stresses the dynamic unity of person and work (p. 309). Both the Old and the New Testaments testify to God's redemption, not as a dissolution of God's creation, but as its completion (p. 214).

Childs is a fine Old Testament scholar and has contributed many erudite and seminal publications on the Old Testament traditions. His presupposition that we must begin with the canon of the church is, however, lamentable. As Christians, we may be sensitive to his position, but ultimately we must part company.[44] To start with a closed canon of the Old and New Testaments is to begin in the fourth century C.E., and perhaps later. It is a long leap from there to the time when the last book in the Christian Bible was completed and when the Old Testament canon was finally closed, specifically some time around the middle of the second century C.E. It is essential to think back two thousand years and to recognize that the New Testament authors had no closed canon[45] and that some documents eventually collected into the New Testament were either not yet written or were circulating only in some communities and only on separate scrolls or slips of papyrus. Equally important, the quotation of 1 Enoch by Jude clarifies that any study of the relation of the Testaments must now include the Jewish Pseudepigrapha and other writings we brand as extracanonical. These documents were certainly considered inspired by many early Jews and Christians. The author of Jude did not consider 1 Enoch "extracanonical," "exotic," or insignificant; he claimed that Enoch had prophesied (*proephēteusen de* . . . *Henōch legōn*; Jude 14) about the coming of "our Lord Jesus Christ" (Jude 17).

In *Torah and Canon* (Philadelphia: Fortress Press, 1972), James Sanders obliquely commented on his view of the relation of the Testaments. For him the origin and essence of the Bible lies in the concept of Torah. He rightly stresses, as does Childs, that we must look holistically at the Bible. We must not seek to establish its unity but to describe its shape and function. He stresses the monotheistic pluralism in the Bible. Sanders focuses our attention so that the study of Torah and canon is a "quest for the essence of the power for life" palpably present in the Bible.[46] He urges us to struggle with the search for the canon within the canon, without losing sight of the full canonical context of our task. For Sanders the New Testament is to be understood, to a certain extent, as a unique type of midrash.

Sanders' work is suggestive and promising. His thought is creative and persuasive, but on some points I must demur. Sanders knows the danger of succumbing to reductionism and looking for only the canon within the canon. To label the New Testament as "midrash" does bring forth its exegetical character; but it tends to misrepresent the uniqueness of "gospel" as a genre peculiar to Christianity, and it confuses the impressive varieties of genre and thought in the New Testament. To state that the Old Testament is the "only ancient authority that the NT writers recognize or cite"[47] certainly shows that the books in the Old Testament are frequently cited as inspired and authoritative to the New Testament authors, but it fails to do justice to the other works cited as inspired by them.[48] As mentioned earlier, Jude quotes as prophecy the Book of Enoch, and this section of 1 Enoch is clearly pre-Christian and Jewish, for the precise quotation in Jude has recently been discovered in an Aramaic fragment of Enoch that dates from the first century B.C.E.[49]

In *The Elusive Presence* (New York: Harper & Row 1978), Samuel Terrien turns our attention to the presence of God as perceived in the Bible. Unlike the gods of other religions, Yahweh cannot be summoned, controlled, or manipulated. Yahweh has made his will known at Sinai, but the Commandments are to guide and control Israel and not God. Terrien stresses that the biblical seers heard God's command "suddenly and unexpectedly."[50] God's presence would overwhelm the senses and then fade, leaving behind "a memory and a hope." The faded presence burned these "into an alloy of inward certitude, which was *emunah*, 'faith.' "[51]

Terrien points out that Old Testament theology cannot be constructed on the covenant motif or on the concepts of "election, kingdom, the self-asseveration 'I-Am-Yahweh,' creation, redemption, community, and eschatology."[52] These comments reveal that Terrien's recognition of the diversity of the Old Testament theologies led him to part company with Eichrodt. He also expressed the difficulty he had with von Rad, stating that Israel's various testimonies cannot be presented as "Old Testament theology."

Terrien argues for canonical continuity between the Testaments. The Old Testament seers were overwhelmed by God's presence and then forced to live with God's elusiveness. Likewise, Jesus' earliest followers experienced his brief historical existence and claimed a postmortem "visionary exaltation"; but each of these "soon faded." Pointing out the vast theological tensions within both the Old and the New Testaments, Terrien urges us to perceive a dynamic center in the Bible. He is convinced that "a legitimate approach to a genuine theology of the entire Bible" might be through "the Hebraic theology of presence."[53] In essence, this understanding reveals a paradox. God's presence must be grasped in God's absence.

Terrien's recognition is insightful and profound. All who have felt God's awesome presence go on to experience the inability to call God to be present again and must yearn for God's next initiative. As Samuel E. Balentine claims, the people of Israel had to struggle with God's "inexplicable divine hiddenness."[54]

A major proof text for Terrien is Isaiah 45:15a: "Verily, thou art a God that hidest thyself!"[55] God is not a hidden God; God is one who has hidden himself. Terrien points out the conceptual theological link between this passage in Isaiah and Jesus' cry of dereliction on the cross, which of course was taken from Psalm 22: "My God, my God, why have you forsaken me?" (v. 1). Terrien goes on to point out that this cry of abandonment is an affirmation of God's presence, because it leads to the plea for God to be "not far" (Ps. 22:11 [Hebrew 22:12]) and culminates with a pledge to proclaim God's name "to my brothers" (22:22 [Hebrew 22:23]).

Terrien has focused his thoughts on the development of an ecumenical theology of the Bible. Essential in that endeavor is a solution to the issue of the relation of the Testaments. For him "the motif of 'the presence of God' " does provide a unifying and yet dynamic principle that will account not only for the homogeneity of the Old Testament literature in its totality, including the sapiential books, but also for the historical and thematic continuity that unites Hebraism and large aspects of Judaism with nascent Christianity.[56]

Terrien has made a major contribution. It is not yet clear to me, however, that the paradox of "presence in absence" is as attuned to the dynamics of biblical thought, faith, and action as it is to the poetic subtleties of contemporary life. I am persuaded that a distinction must be made between being overcome by God's presence theophanically and being aware of God's presence phenomenologically. To speak about "presence in absence"—as attractive and profound as that sounds—is to move precariously away from phenomena to noumena. Such a tendency veers away from the realm of biblical theology.

The biblical men and women tend to become actors and actresses similar to the mythical ones in Plato's cave. Are not the biblical actors attractive because they are not model people, but are so earthy, real, and often flawed? Joshua's spies visit Rahab while they are in Jericho, and she is a harlot. David founds the nation Israel, but falls for the beautiful wife of Uriah. The Bible is full of the most beautiful poetry in the world, but it is not a book of poetry. It records in celebrated language and edited traditions reflections on how God had been remembered as present to men and women of clay.

Did the pilgrims to the holy sites and the worshipers in the Temple cult not feel and experience the presence of God? Does not Psalm 46 record the experience of those who confessed the presence of God?[57] Did not the annual feasts and even the daily meals in the homes of the devout not have a celebration of God's presence? Was not God experienced in a recitation of God's mighty deeds? Did not even the apocalyptists stress the presence of God, affirming almost everywhere in the extant apocalypses that God does hear prayers? Are not the angels to confirm the connection, not the separation, of the heavenly and earthly realms?[58]

God's presence is indeed elusive in a profound sense.[59] But is that not because of human sin, finiteness, and the ontological difference between Creator and creatures? After theophanies, is God not still present in memory and hope? After Jesus ascends into heaven, according to the author of Luke-Acts, is not the emphasis placed upon continuing presence through the unparalleled, yet continuing, power of the Holy Spirit? To what extent is Terrien's concept of elusive presence parallel to Philo of

Alexandria's insight that we apprehend no attribute of God save God's existence (*The Unchangeableness of God* 61–62) and that no name, utterance, or conception is adequate to comprehend God (*On Dreams* 1.67)? Are not analogical reasoning and finite human language poor means of articulating the presence and elusiveness of God? Terrien's thoughts are stimulating; he has urged us to proceed along a very promising path.

Biblical scholars have served us well. We now know in profound ways that the Christian Bible is full of diverse and complex theological reflections and affirmations. These are conditioned by a time far into the past and by a place unalterably changed and far removed from us. It is impossible, and undesirable, to systematize either the Old or the New Testament. It is difficult to perceive a dynamic center or even a canon within the canon. It is evident that the Testaments cannot be faithfully represented under the traditional umbrella of promise and fulfillment. Where are we now today? Are the Testaments related in any way, or are we left with recognizing discontinuities, differences, and diversities?

Three Questions

Three questions help organize the final part of this essay, as we turn now from a report and critique of research to an attempt to try to refine additional suggestions for discerning how and in what ways, if at all, the Testaments are related. We have already seen that each of the major attempts has at least something to contribute; hence, we should not search in vain for the one solution to this continuing perplexing problem.

First, let us seek to discern if there is a missing link in the Jewish history and literature that comes generally from the period between the Testaments. Second, let us explore more fully how that literature helps us understand the movement of language, thought, and theology from the Old Testament to the New Testament. Third, let us ponder the question, How are the Testaments related for us who are living at the end of the second millennium?

Is there a missing link? Scholars have shown some of the ways that the Testaments can be related, but a link has been missing in these discussions.[60] The Testaments are indeed separated by over two hundred years: Daniel, the latest Old Testament book, was written before 160 B.C.E., and 1 Thessalonians, the earliest book in the New Testament, was written after 40 C.E. This time was not a period of silence, and it is not necessary to try to leap over the centuries. We do have now over 65 Old Testament Pseudepigrapha, 13 Old Testament Apocrypha, 170 Dead Sea Scrolls, and numerous letters and archaeological discoveries that cumulatively link chronologically Daniel with Thessalonians. These discoveries are essential in any attempt to discern the relations of the Testaments.

We are now in possession of hundreds of hymns and prayers composed during this so-called intertestamental period;[61] indeed, we now have two hymnbooks—the Psalms of Solomon and the Hodayoth—and a Qumran Psalter that is different in order and sometimes content from the Davidic psalms in the Masoretic Bible, which lies behind all English translations of the psalms.

Equally important is the relation of Jesus' followers to the Hebrew Scriptures. They did not read them in a vacuum or in light of modern, usually German insights. Edward Schillebeeckx astutely set forth the following argument:

> Scholars are so often inclined to make much of the Old Testament, whereas Judaism . . . particularly that of Jesus' own time, is presented in a distorted fashion. As a result, the relation between Jesus and Judaism is itself distorted; one forgets that the Old Testament was not functioning *per se* or in isolation but in the context of late Jewish piety as that had since been developing. One cannot with

impunity skip over the time that had elapsed between the great prophets and Jesus.[62]

Although these comments were not tendered to explain the relation of the Testaments, they are obviously essential to this task. Our search for the relation of the Testaments will be enriched if we keep in focus the fact that Jesus and the authors of the New Testament read what we call the Old Testament in the context of Early Judaism, which was vibrantly alive and attuned to the continuing power of God's word recorded in Torah.

Two points in particular should now be before us in the continuing search for the relation of the Testaments. First, the importance of Early Judaism, including Jesus' Judaism, and the interpretation of the Scriptures in his time are essential dimensions of our work. Second, we must not falsify early Jewish thought or ignore the continuity of piety and faithfulness of many Jews during the beginnings of Christianity.

The new discoveries of documents from Jesus' time help create a renewed appreciation of Judaism and of the Jews in our communities. In the fall of 1989, scholars gathered in Princeton to discuss Paul's attitude to "the Jews." Many speakers stressed Paul's pride in being a Jew and his claim that God has not nullified God's promises or canceled God's covenant with the Jews (Rom. 11:1–2).[63] In the air were thoughts about the possibility of recognizing two covenants: the old one made between God and God's chosen people, and the new one made through Jesus.[64]

Such possibilities for discourse and open reflection were simply not possible in Germany during the professorial careers of Eichrodt, von Rad, and Bultmann. They provided the presuppositions, agenda, and vision for biblical research in Europe, the United States, and in many other countries. In Israel, at least one voice, unfortunately only in Hebrew, was brilliantly, if idiosyncratically, writing an appreciably different history of the religion of Israel. Yehezkel Kaufmann argued that the Wellhausenist approach was erroneous, and claimed that Israelite religion was unaffected by "paganism."[65] In 1929 and 1930, in his *Golah ve-Nekhar* (*Exile and Estrangement*) (Hebrew City, Jerusalem: Magnes Press), Kaufmann struggled with the difference between Judaism and Christianity, and pondered the possibility of two distinct covenants. (Chapters of this work, titled *Christianity and Judaism*, have been translated by C. W. Efroymson and published in 1988 by the Magnes Press of the Hebrew University, Jerusalem.)

Living in a pluralistic society demands developing a position that can be defended academically. Our students and graduates should be able publicly to clarify a mature and reflective argument. Emotional attachment to faith has in the past sometimes misled us into presenting arguments that were not carefully developed and even false. In our traditions are, *inter alia*, honest, informed, and enlightened reflections that can assist us in the perennial Christian search to understand the relation of the Testaments.

Jews are living among us, and many continue in faithful worship and obedience to the God we share. They are interested in our problems, and they would want our deliberations to be informed. They also are searching to discern how the Hebrew Scriptures—or Old Testament—are related to the Mishnah and later compilations. Our task today seems more complex and frustrating than it was decades ago. Many of the attempts in the past are no longer viable in light of the advances in the humanities, and especially in biblical research.

We are now able to raise the second question: How does the early Jewish literature help us comprehend the movement of language, thought, and theology from the Old Testament to the New Testament? To begin with, what significant light is now shown upon the concept of the Messiah? The claim that Jesus is "the Messiah" is understandable only within Jewish culture, and in light of the Old Testament to a certain extent, but of most importance in view of the early Jewish writings contemporaneous with or somewhat earlier than the Gospels. The term "messiah" in the Old Testament does not denote God's final agent in the history of salvation. In the Old Testament books, "messiah" is used of king, priest, and prophet.

In the books that link the Old and New Testaments, "messiah" is sometimes used to denote the one who is to be sent by God to bring to completion the final acts in the drama of salvation.[66] The New Testament concept of "the Messiah" is linked with the Old Testament through the theology of Early Judaism. Here again we observe that any discussion of the relation of the Testaments must include the so-called intertestamental writings.

"Son of God" and even "Son of the Most High" have now appeared in one of the Dead Sea Scrolls, the so-called Pseudo-Daniel (4Qps Dan A).[67] In this late first-century B.C.E. Aramaic text, these terms are applied to an unknown human being. Although the document is preserved only in fragments, it probably is an apocalyptic Jewish work that probably had messianic overtones.[68] The concept of "Son of God" in early Jewish literature helps link some Old Testament passages in which it denotes a divine being with many New Testament pericopes.

Contrary to Bultmann's claim that "Son of God" in early Christianity evolved under the influence of the mystery religions,[69] the major development of Christology from Jesus to Paul occurred within Judaism, as J. D. G. Dunn,[70] Leonhard Goppelt, Martin Hengel, Ernst Käsemann, C. F. D. Moule, Willi Marxsen, others, and I have endeavored to show.[71] These observations significantly help to reveal how the New is related through early Jewish theology to the Old Testament.

The term "Son of Man" is almost always found only in sayings of Jesus in the New Testament. Most New Testament scholars now conclude that some of these derive ultimately from Jesus himself. Hence, Jesus used the term

"Son of Man." Now we must ask, What did it mean to
Jesus and what did it mean in the theology of his time? In
this endeavor it is enlightening to discover that the
term—and perhaps title—is found in a document that is
now admitted to be not only Jewish but also Palestinian
and contemporaneous with and perhaps earlier than
Jesus. The document is the pseudepigraphical Parables of
Enoch (1 Enoch 37–71).

To discover what Jesus and his followers—and the
authors of the New Testament—meant by "the Son of
Man" takes us not primarily to Ezekiel and Daniel in the
Old Testament. It leads to the early Jewish writings, especially the Pseudepigrapha (1 Enoch 37–71 and 4 Ezra 13).
Any discussion of the relation of the Testaments would be
enriched by this fact. These Jewish writings are not the
missing link in a chain, but they help link the Old and the
New Testaments.

The Old and the New are coupled also by means of
the varieties for interpreting the "Scriptures," the Old
Testament. The Old Testament Scriptures and early Jewish religious writings provided the perceptions and the
methods to interpret the major events experienced by
Jesus' followers. This is abundantly clear when we reexamine the crucifixion and resurrection of Jesus, and
surely these two events are the most significant ones in
salvation history for the Christian. How then are we to
understand them? Why did Jesus suffer crucifixion? Why
did his earliest followers proclaim that he had been raised
by God? What language and conceptual categories
enabled these claims to be chosen, articulated, and considered meaningful discourse by the opponents of the
Jesus Group and of the Peter Group?

The crucifixion of Jesus is one of the unassailable
facts of Jesus' life. Atheists, agnostics, Jews, and
extremely liberal Christians—as well as Christian fundamentalists and conservatives—accept it as a historical
fact. Jesus' earliest followers clearly understood it as the
end to a majestic career of full obedience to God. Cleopas'

disappointment placards this mood and comprehension: "We had hoped that he was the one" (Luke 24:21). How, then, did Jesus' followers come to grasp that the crucifixion was Jesus' finest hour, and, in the words of the author of the Gospel of John, his exaltation (John 13:32)?

Surely, this understanding appeared only after the disciples became convinced that Jesus was resurrected by God. Hence, the experience of the resurrected Jesus was obviously the most powerful force for the paradigm shift from allegiance to a Galilean who ended his life on the cross to worship through and even to the One who now reigns in heaven.

It has not been possible to point to the concept of a "suffering Messiah" in early Jewish thought. The Jews who followed Jesus could not simply make an easy equation between him and some concept in Jewish theology.[72]

The Jews who followed Jesus could appeal to the Jewish theology of sacrifice and especially the binding of Isaac (the Akedah). The powerfully symbolic binding of Isaac for sacrifice is found, of course, in the Elohistic stratum of the Pentateuch (Genesis 22). The earliest Christians, like Paul and the author of Hebrews, were dependent on this text primarily through the Jewish understanding and exegetical interpretations of it in Jubilees 17, Philo (On Abraham), Pseudo-Philo (18, 23, 32, 40), 4 Maccabees (6, 7, 13, 16, 17), Josephus (*Antiquities* 1), and the early traditions behind the Palestinian Targumim.[73] Surely, the Testaments are linked along such rich traditions in Early Jewish exegesis.[74]

Jesus' early followers also had the benefit of the Jewish exegetical reflections on the concept of the suffering servant in Isaiah 53. As is well known, Jesus' followers interpreted this text prophetically as pointing to Jesus. He was then seen as God's servant, a transition that was relatively easy to make—but only in Greek and not in Semitics[75]—for *pais theou* denotes not only "servant of God" but also "child of God." The conception of Jesus as God's Son, which I have tried to show derives from Jesus' own self-understanding,[76] would have laid the basis for the comprehension. The Christology of the New Testament is thus seen to be linked with the Old Testament through Jesus' words and the traditions of Early Judaism.

The crucifixion was seen as the death of "the Righteous One," which was a title for Jesus, according to Acts, the Odes of Solomon, and other Christian texts. This title is now found to be Jewish, pre-Christian, and Palestinian, for it is found in the Parables of Enoch (1 Enoch 37–71). Because the title "the Righteous One" is equated with "the Messiah" in this Jewish document,[77] it is evident that there were Jewish concepts, terms, titles, and symbols that the Jewish followers of Jesus knew. These would help them to conceptualize the crucifixion. Obviously, the seeds for sowing a more meaningful explanation of the relation of the Testaments must be sown in the fertile thoughts of early Jewish theology, which was grounded on the sacred Scriptures called the Old Testament.

Jesus' resurrection was unexpected, and there was no developed Jewish myth about the appearance of one who had been resurrected that would help remove the scandalous nature of the early proclamation. Cleopas thought the Jesus dream was shattered (Luke 24:21). Mary Magdalene reputedly asked someone she thought was a gardener where Jesus' corpse had been placed (John 20:15).

When Jesus' resurrection by God was experienced, it was possible, however, to proclaim this event because Jews had been developing the concept of resurrection and the related cosmology from about the third century B.C.E. The concept of resurrection, so important for New Testament theology, was developed not in the Old Testament, but in the intertestamental writings.[78]

Here most emphatically a search for an understanding of the relation of the Testaments confronts the fact that sometimes Jewish literature is more important for bridging, or clarifying, the relationship than is the Old Testament. The authors of the Old Testament books customarily look for the resurrection of the *nation* Israel. Only one very late passage clearly denotes the belief in the resurrection of the *individual* from the dead—Daniel 12.

Here we must ask the following: Did Jews just prior to and sometimes contemporaneous with Jesus not interpret many of the Old Testament passages anachronistically, as many Christians do today? Did they not also read their belief in the resurrection of the dead back into earlier Scriptures? The answer to both questions is certainly "yes." This hermeneutic was possible because Palestinian Jews, by the time of Jesus, stressed that there was life after death and that God resurrected the deceased individual. According to the author of 2 Maccabees, Razis threw his internal organs at his enemies and cried out that he will get them back in the resurrection (2 Macc. 14:46). The earliest reference to the Jewish belief in the resurrection of the dead is in a Jewish document many decades earlier than Daniel 12. It is 1 Enoch 1–36. The major Jewish synagogal prayer—the Amidah, or Eighteen Benedictions, which was recited widely in Palestine during the time of Jesus—records the deep-seated Jewish belief in the resurrection. In the second benediction, God is praised; God is the one who sustains the living and resurrects the dead.[79]

We know that some of Jesus' followers believed in the resurrection of the dead. At least one of them misinterpreted the possibility of Lazarus' resurrection by comprehending his resurrection not in the presence of Jesus' earthly life but in terms of the resurrection of the dead at the end of time (John 11:24). Paul uses the belief in a resurrection from the dead to divide the court that is about to judge him (Acts 23:6). He claims that if Christ has not been raised from the dead Jesus' followers are to be pitied (1 Cor. 15:18).

These observations reveal once again that a bridge to relate the Testaments is not to be constructed over a chasm of centuries. The relation is bridged by Jewish religious documents composed during these centuries. Any discussion of the relation of the Testaments must no longer simply repeat the New Testament authors' use of the paradigm of promise-fulfillment. All our reflections and discussions must now be informed by the perception that the Jews who wrote the New Testament works lived in a culture that provided religious language and conception for comprehending and proclaiming Jesus as the One-who-was-to-come. Along with many other Jews, including the authors of the Dead Sea Scrolls and some Pseudepigrapha, Jesus' followers saw their own time as the period for the fulfillment of God's promises.

Let me try to put this perception once again into focus. Many New Testament theologians are stressing[80] that Christian theology is profoundly shaped by Jewish apocalyptic thought.[81] This understanding, in its basic perception, is accurate; hence, the link between Old and New is not only between Daniel and Revelation, but also between many passages in the Old Testament and Mark 13 and other apocalyptic passages in the New Testament, and indeed the whole apocalyptic and eschatological ground and expectation of the New Testament. Most assuredly, these links must be seen in light of the numerous Jewish apocalypses and apocalyptic works that are roughly contemporaneous with Jesus and his followers.

All of the above enable us to move with control to our third question, which obviously has been with us all along: What is the relation of the Testaments for Christians today? Surely, some Christians act, if not think, that the Old is old and to be discarded. Some may want to interpret Paul so as to stress that "everything old has passed away; see, everything has become new!" (2 Cor. 5:17), without perceiving that in Romans 9–11, and elsewhere, Paul saw the continuing importance of Scripture (the Old Testament).

Many preachers continue without justification or examination to read the Old Testament as if it were written by clairvoyants who saw Jesus as the Christ or as if the prophets were the first Christians. Perhaps our first task is to point out the impossibility of that position. The Old Testament works are misunderstood if they are interpreted anachronistically and christologically.

In the search for truth and understanding, it is painfully difficult to pay full allegiance to the results of intensive biblical research and the continuing power and validity of the witnesses in the New Testament. Augustine, Luther, Barth, and other leading theologians never condoned sacrificing, or even compromising, scholarship for faith. The two are not paradigmatically antithetical.

We may admit that the concept of promise and fulfillment will not serve Christians today as it did the first believers two thousand years ago, but is it totally bankrupt for us? I do not think a Christian who believes in any way that Jesus is the One-who-was-to-come can say "yes" to that question. Can it be modified? I am convinced it can be.

As sound scholars and preachers have stressed for years, the prophets were not promising the coming of Jesus Christ. His life and teaching, however, can be comprehended only in light of some of their understandings of God, the purposefulness of history, and the promise—or dream—of a future day when God will be King and God's kingdom will come on earth. There is no direct and obvious line of development from the prophets to Jesus, but the Old Testament prophetic books are essential sources for the proclamation of the salvific meaning of his life and thought.

Have we accurately grasped the relation between prophecy and proclamation by the terms "promise" and "fulfillment"? Fulfillment does fit some of the New Testament writers, even if, as Bultmann showed, they read "into them what they already know"; [82] but does "promise" adequately represent the words of the prophets? How can we know that the prophets are looking to a far distant future and not, as so often seems to be the case, to a promise that is expected in their own time or in the near future?[83] Does "promise" not imply to a general reader that the prophets were passing on the words of God about events five hundred or more years into the future? Can preachers ignore what biblical scholarship has clarified—that the prophets' words were shaped by the needs of their own times?

I am convinced that a way can be found by replacing "promise" with "expectation." This term may help us avoid the unattractive meanings popularly associated with "promise" and the demands possibly made upon God (*deus ex machina*) as one who can, as in the Jewish Magical Papyri, be controlled because of the promises that fetter him (*quid pro quo*).

"Expectation" may also be better than "promise" because, as many biblical theologians have shown, the expectation that God will act soon to save[84] God's people permeates the theologies (and liturgies) of Israel and Judaism. It better represents the prophets' foretelling[85] proclamations, which often begin with the formula "thus says Yahweh". This formula of expectation was not meant for some far distant future; it was customarily addressed to the contemporaries of the prophet. The term "expectation" also better represents the development of Old Testament theology in the direction of apocalypticism, which was obviously not a linear movement. Generally speaking, expectation helps clarify the broad development from Old to New: Old Testament theology concludes with apocalyptic eschatology. Intertestamental Judaism is apocalyptic. And New Testament theology is grounded in Israelite and Jewish apocalyptic thought and apocalypticism.[86]

The paradigm does not seem to be promise-fulfillment; perhaps it might be *expectation-proclamation*. If so, the proclamation cannot merely be derived from, or evolved from, the prophets. The element of creativity, of the unexpected, and of the shockingly new must be allowed.[87] It certainly operated in the lives of the disciples, who were at a loss for comprehending Jesus' essen-

tial message. Any discussion of the relation of the
Testaments must assuredly be informed of the new
dimensions of "Jesus research" and the insight that his
disciples were not prepared for his unique synthesis of
traditions and his reordering of them in light of the powers being manifest through him.

This recognition does not necessarily denote succumbing to unbridled, if sophisticated, confessionalism.
Jews are now very much involved in Jesus research, as is
clear in the collection of essays in *Jesus' Jewishness*.[88]

Typological interpretation is also possible,[89] as both
von Rad and Eichrodt successfully, in different ways,
showed.[90] Perhaps it can be reconceptualized in light of
its varied use in the intertestamental writings, but it cannot be derived without modification from the simple relation of the Testaments assumed by many New Testament
authors. Typology should be used with careful critical
controls and in light of a refined perception of the relation
of the Testaments. Typology should be brought into the
discussion near the conclusion of a detailed assessment of
how the Testaments are related. Typology extends from
images or symbols—such as lamb, king, shepherd—to
the casting of narratives as types of earlier stories; for
example, the Joseph story clearly shaped the Daniel
story.[91]

It will continue to be valid and illuminating for Chris-
tians to portray Jesus typologically as the lamb slain by
Abraham or the lambs sacrificed in the Temple cult, as the
just king with wisdom like Solomon, as the shepherd like
David who knows how to love his flock, and as the
Joseph who suffered for—and saved—his loved ones.

Each of these types is grounded in the Old Testament
narrative and also developed in early Jewish literature.
For example, the lamb symbolism at Passover time is
enriched by the sign of the lamb's salvific blood developed in Jubilees 49; the wise king typology is deepened
by the messianic interpretation supplied by the author of
the Psalms of Solomon 17 and 18; the shepherd imagery

is employed to explain the history of God's people from the Flood to the messianic kingdom after the Maccabean wars by the author of 1 Enoch 89 to 90; and the Joseph typology is expanded in diverse and complex ways by the authors of the Testaments of the Twelve Patriarchs and Joseph and Aseneth. The authors of the New Testament books inherited the typology developed by their Jewish ancestors and contemporaries.

It is clear that typology was used by Jews long before Paul and the evangelists. The Dead Sea Scrolls and the Pseudepigrapha provide additional models for the typological and symbolical interpretation of Scriptures and traditions. We can learn from these ancient texts, both ways not to do typology and possible methods and typologies to try. For example, to refer to God's planting brings a typological relation between the Hodayoth (1QH 8) and Isaiah (Isaiah 5), and also between many of Jesus' parables and Isaiah. Jesus probably can be seen in terms of royal images, especially the elevation of Israel's king to sonship with God, a thought that is expressed in the Old Testament, especially in Psalm 2:

> "I have set my king on Zion, my holy hill."
> I will tell of the decree of the LORD:
> He said to me, "You are my son;
>   Today I have begotten you." (Ps. 2:6–7)

Theologically, we are supplied with some biblical control for considering the typological meaning of Jesus' "sonship."[92] Typology is one of the important ways the Testaments are related, and again this relation is often brought into clear focus by the theologies and technical terms of intertestamental Judaism. This dimension of the New Testament is obvious in Hebrews, whose author mastered the Jewish use of typology.

The relation of the Testaments becomes clearer through a recognition of the way God is said to come to God's people; and, of course, the dimension is historical—how God *has come* in space and time to God's own people according to Scripture. God appears in history and speaks the language of those who hear God. Paul Hanson has recently pointed to a unifying dimension within the vast diversity of the various biblical books; the "common grounding" is "in the one true God, whose purpose throughout time is one."[93] The biblical authors affirmed that God had been experienced in past and present deeds, by visions and dreams, and especially through the word spoken by the prophet. The authors of the Old and the New Testaments affirm this selfsame character of God, means of reaching God's creation, and purpose in history.

Unfortunately, it is not sufficiently appreciated that the biblical authors comprehended God as "awesome."[94] This term is a neglected key for opening a door through which we may see another dimension of the relation of the Testaments.

The first of the Eighteen Benedictions praises the "God of our Fathers" as an "awesome God." One of the recently published Dead Sea Scrolls is a hymn on the awesomeness of God; 4Q381 50, line 3, calls upon God as "awe-inspiring." Such non-Christian insights give us some objectivity for linking the Testaments. From the creation, described in Genesis through to the latest psalms in the Psalter, God is celebrated in God's awesomeness. The author of Job highlights this incomprehensible dimension of the one and the same God who stands behind both the Old and New Testaments. It is significant that Paul, in his focused discussion of God's history of salvation with the Jews, urges the Gentiles to "stand in awe" (Rom. 11:20). The author of 4 Ezra calls upon God to remember those who have known "awe" of him (4 Ezra 8:20).

According to the evangelists, on one occasion a boat was filling with water and the disciples pleaded for Jesus to calm the storm. He is said to have calmed the wind and the waves. Then the disciples were described as filled with "awe" (Mark 4:41). The essence of biblical theology and the heart of Christology is the same—an inarticulate wonder at God's *awesomeness.*

Conclusion

No one solution explains adequately the relation of the Testaments. As James Barr stressed, the relation of the Testaments is extremely complex.[95] The task is not easy; it demands penetrating reflection. To struggle to comprehend the relation of the Old and the New Testaments is a necessary responsibility for every educated Christian. It is a fruitful task. Christians have both Testaments. The Old is not to be jettisoned, interpreted christologically, seen as a history of failure, or uprooted out of its social settings.

Four major developments explored in this essay help us improve the solutions presented by Eichrodt, von Rad, and Bultmann: (1) Full consideration is to be given to the pivotal significance of the so-called intertestamental "sacred" writings. (2) The ancient Scriptures were not read in a vacuum by the followers of Jesus. Almost all were Jews, and they read the Scriptures (the Old Testament) within the exegetical ambience of Early Judaism. (3) Our attempts to explain how the two Testaments are related must be done with a perception of the Jews, who continue to be faithful to Torah, in our academies and communities. (4) We have gained a deeper understanding of the linguistic and conceptual background and foreground of the New Testament authors. Let me very briefly explain each of these points.

First, the search for the relation of the Testaments includes all of the sixty-six canonical writings and also the hundreds of sacred extrabiblical intertestamental documents that clearly bridge the chronological chasm between the Testaments. These documents were often deemed to be inspired by many of Jesus' followers.

Second, our struggle to comprehend the relation of the Testaments is enlightened by the fact that Jesus and his earliest followers did not read the ancient Scriptures with the benefit of modern historical criticism. For them the Pentateuch was written by Moses, the prophets quoted God infallibly, and the expectations of the prophets were being fulfilled in their midst.

The members of the Palestinian Jesus Movement were able to benefit from their contemporaries' creative approaches to Scripture and the impressive freedom showed in shaping, even altering, texts.[96] Jesus' early followers, like the devotees of the Righteous Teacher who founded the community that produced the Dead Sea Scrolls, were not forced to interpret in a mechanical way the ancient Scriptures. They were freed by life with him, life in the creative world of Early Judaism, and the invigorating power of Jesus' resurrection to express with astonishing freedom the meaning of the New in light of the Old. Obviously, the relation they saw was through a type of messianic exegesis.[97]

Third, our attempts to relate the Testaments need to be informed of the reverence accorded the *Tanakh*—the Christian's Old Testament—by Jews in our communities today.[98] Jews have for centuries held fast to the paradigm of "the fulfillment" of God's covenantal promises.[99] Expectations were contradicted by past and present experiences, but many Jews hold resolutely to the absolute certainty of *geulah*, the ultimate redemption of God's elect. As Moshe Weinfeld has clarified, "The belief in a final revelation of God to save the world thus unites all Israelite sources, from the prayer of Moses to the contemporary liturgy."[100] In antiquity, the Jews gathered on Sabbaths and festivals, praying collectively to God, saying, "We are expecting your coming. . . . Do not tarry, even if you tarry we shall wait."[101] As Raphael J. Zwi Werblowsky stresses, Israel's ultimate redemption "was not a matter of hope but of absolute certainty."[102]

Fourth, the comprehension of the relation of the Testaments is improved by our increased understanding of the sociology of knowledge, the phenomenology of language, and Paul Ricoeur's insights regarding the method and the interest that "rules the historical method."[103] We must endeavor to be so imbued with both Testaments, and so-called intertestamental writings, that we do not retroject unexamined popular conceptions, but struggle to grasp the multifaceted relationship.

The language of the New Testament is not a new creation; it is the crystallization of the living language used in Jewish circles in which the Old Testament was the sacred word of God. Hence, Revelation, for example, does not quote one full verse of the Old Testament, but the Semitic-Greek of the author alludes to the Old Testament in almost 75 percent of its verses.[104]

Because our Western civilization is "a historical civilization" and because our self-understanding is dependent upon some understanding of our predecessors, it is imperative to grasp how the originators of the Christian faith went about relating Scriptures to the present. For them the process entailed interpreting traditions—almost always the Old Testament—in a living, eschatologically charged social setting, often not far from the smoke of sacrifice in the Temple.

Christianity, it is clear, must not be defined as a religion divorced from its origins. Christianity not only inherited the Scriptures of the Jews; it was formed both by the Jewish means of interpreting these sacred works and by Jesus and his earliest followers, all of whom were Jews. And the interpretation occurred within Judaism; the earliest decades of Christianity, and perhaps its first one hundred years, were spent *within, then alongside of, Judaism.*

We have sixty-six canonical books; all must be included in the struggle for comprehension of the relation—which, of course, is a chronological one, from the thirty-nine to the twenty-seven, and to the comprehensive sixty-six. To relate them demands perceiving the link of hundreds of intertestamental works that bridge the times that separate the twenty-seven from the thirty-nine.

Seeking the relation of the Testaments must be informed by the difficulty of relating Ecclesiastes with Deuteronomy or Romans with James. Surely, in some senses those problems may be more difficult than relating the New Testament to the Old.

Scholars have also warned against approaching the Bible, especially the Old Testament, as if our task is to supply proof texts. The Bible is not a quarry for infallible dogmas; it must not be reduced to the role of providing proofs for truths obtained by other means.[105]

The fulfillment of the expectation is the appearance of the divine person through God's *continuing grace*. For the Christian, Jesus Christ is Immanuel, God's designated Lord of history and time (Philippians 2). This confession demands recognizing the fundamental importance of the Old for the New.

The theology of awe helps us grasp the Christology of awe. The *mysterium tremendum* is an experience of the personal power who has been experienced and heard by the faithful from Abraham to Ezra, from Ezra to Hillel and Jesus, from Jesus to John, and from them to the faithful in synagogues and churches today.[106]

Notes

1. See the discussion of Rudolf Bultmann and his reflections on the promise-fulfillment paradigm. I want to express appreciation for discussions with my colleague, Patrick D. Miller, Charles T. Haley Professor of Old Testament Theology.

2. Walther Zimmerli, "Promise and Fulfillment," in *Essays on Old Testament Hermeneutics*, ed. Claus Westermann, trans. James L. Mays (Richmond: John Knox Press, 1964), 89–122, esp. 91, 95.

3. An early Christian composed a document in which

"Isaiah son of Amoz" saw the virgin Mary and the carpenter Joseph. While both were "alone" Mary saw "a small infant." Isaiah is then reported to have seen Jesus' miracles, crucifixion, and resurrection. See the Martyrdom and Ascension of Isaiah, esp. ch. 11, in *The Old Testament Pseudepigrapha*, vol. 2, ed. James H. Charlesworth (New York: Doubleday, 1985), 174–176.

4. It is obviously difficult for Christians to acknowledge that Jesus did not fulfill most of the alleged messianic promises. He did not free God's people from the Romans. He did not bring in the end of time or open the gates to Paradise.

5. See the excellent collection of essays edited by Hershel Shanks in *Ancient Israel: A Short History from Abraham to the Roman Destruction of the Temple* (Washington, D.C.: Biblical Archaeology Society 1988).

6. Walther Eichrodt, *Theology of the Old Testament*, 2 vols. trans. J. A. Baker (Philadelphia: Westminster Press, 1961, 1967), 1:26.

7. Patrick D. Miller informs me that he thinks it is quite likely that covenant was known in Hosea's time and possibly before. Recognizing that the best sources for the concept of the covenant postdate Moses by centuries, Delbert R. Hillers nevertheless rejects Wellhausen's late dating of the covenant. He argues that we should not assume that Israel "started from nothing" and that the covenant with Yahweh "makes it possible to explain how the twelve tribes of Israel lived together before there was a king in Israel." Hillers, *Covenant: The History of a Biblical Idea* (Baltimore: Johns Hopkins Press, 1969), 68.

8. Patrick D. Miller, "Wellhausen as Historian of Religion," in *Julius Wellhausen and His Prolegomena to the History of Israel* (Semeia 25; Chico, Calif.: Scholars Press, 1983), 61–73; and Miller, "Israelite Religion," in *The Hebrew Bible and Its Modern Interpreters*, ed. Douglas A. Knight and Gene M. Tucker (Chico, Calif.: Scholars Press, 1985), 201–237; esp. 223.

9. Eichrodt, *Theology of the Old Testament*, 1:18, cf. p. 66.

10. E. P. Sanders has argued that the essence of Early Judaism was "covenantal nomism" and that concept is a major link between Paul and Jewish traditions. Sanders was not discussing the relation of the Testaments, but he does underscore the importance of the covenant in Early Judaism. Sanders, *Paul and Palestinian Judaism: A Comparison of Patterns of Religion* (Philadelphia: Fortress Press 1977).

11. Gerhard von Rad, *Old Testament Theology*, 2 vols., trans. D. M. G. Stalker (New York: Harper & Row, 1962, 1965), 1:112.

12. Ibid., 2:374.

13. Ibid., 2:353.

14. Ibid., 2:372.

15. Ibid., 2:321.

16. Ibid., 2:384. In my judgment, von Rad's substitution of "prefigurations" for "predictions" is a major improvement in that it provides for the different historical settings of the Old Testament persons, the New Testament persons, and ourselves.

17. Ibid., 2:374.

18. We need a relation of the Testaments that is not exposed as anachronistic or foolish by our Jewish colleagues.

19. Von Rad, *Old Testament Theology*, 2:371.

20. Rudolf Bultmann, "The Significance of the Old Testament for the Christian Faith," in *The Old Testament and Christian Faith*, ed. Bernhard W. Anderson (New York, London: Harper & Row, 1963), 13.

21. Ibid., 34.

22. See Chapter 1 of this volume. See also Bernhard W. Anderson, ed., *The Old Testament and Christian Faith* (New York, London: Harper & Row, 1963).

23. Anderson, ed., "The New Covenant and the Old," in *The Old Testament and Christian Faith*, 225–242.

24. In attempting to be fair to Bultmann and the ethos in which he spent his early years as a professor, we must be careful to discern the date of a publication. Bultmann did write that a "people whose King is God cannot actually tolerate any earthly king," but this statement was not made at the risk of life. It was published in 1949. See Bultmann, "Prophecy and Fulfillment," in Westermann, ed., *Essays on Old Testament Hermeneutics*, 68.

25. Rudolf Bultmann, *Existence and Faith: Shorter Writings of Rudolf Bultmann*, trans. Schubert M. Ogden (Living Age Books 29; New York: Meridian Books, Inc. 1960), 165.

26. See Morris Ashcraft, *Rudolf Bultmann* (Makers of the Modern Theological Mind; Waco, Tex.: Word Books, 1972), 18.

27. Bultmann wrote: "I must mention that my work during the Hitler regime was fructified by the struggle of the church. I have belonged to the Confessing Church since its founding in 1934. Bultmann, *Existence and Faith*, 288. See Norman Perrin, "Life, Times and Work of Rudolf Bultmann," in *The Promise of Bultmann* (Philadelphia: Lippincott; Fortress Press, 1979 1969), 12–17.

28. This declaration rejected the tendencies of the Nazi German Christians; it affirmed, *inter alia*, that the church was

founded on God's revelation in Jesus Christ and not on any other so-called revelation in nature or history.

29. Walther Schmithals, *An Introduction to the Theology of Rudolf Bultmann*, trans. John Bowden (London: 1968), 296–299.

30. See Hans Jonas, "Is Faith Still Possible? Memories of Rudolf Bultmann and Reflections on the Philosophical Aspects of His Work," *HTR* 75 (1982): 1–23.

31. See the judicious comments in defense of Bultmann by John Painter in *Theology as Hermeneutics: Rudolf Bultmann's Interpretation of the History of Jesus* (Sheffield, Eng.: JSOT Press Almond, 1987), esp. 2.

32. Bultmann, "The Significance of the Old Testament for the Christian Faith," in Anderson, ed., *The Old Testament and Christian Faith*, 15.

33. Bultmann, "Prophecy and Fulfillment," in Westermann, ed., *Essays on Old Testament Hermeneutics*, 55.

34. Ibid., 58.

35. Ibid., esp. 58, 72, 74. See also W. Harrelson's lucid essay in Knight and Tucker, eds., *The Hebrew Bible and Its Modern Interpreters*, 489–505. Walter Harrelson points out that Israel's reduced commitment to their Lord and none other elicited widely expressed suspicions that God's people "will fail, and perhaps fail miserably, in embodying and keeping vividly alive this way of life to which they are committed" (p. 497).

36. Zimmerli claimed that the Old Testament is a failure of legalistic attempts to approach God, of any ethnic "prerogatives of Israel based upon the law," and of a covenant "grounded upon the law alone." But he rejects Bultmann's idea that the Old Testament history is one of failure: "Is there not fulfillment here, even in the midst of the shattering?" Walther Zimmerli, "Promise and Fulfillment," in Westermann, ed., *Essays on Old Testament Hermeneutics*, 119. Jews will obviously disagree with Zimmerli's observations regarding failures in the Old Testament. See also Rolf Rendtorff, "Hermeneutik des Alten Testaments als Frage nach der Geschichte," *ZTK* 57 (1960): 27–40.

37. Romans 11:1: "I ask, then, has God rejected his people? By no means!" See the excellent and important discussion of Paul's view of God's promises to God's own people in D. L. Migliore, ed., *The Church and Israel: Romans 9–11* (The Princeton Seminary Bulletin Supplementary Issue 1; Princeton: Princeton University Press, 1990).

38. Bultmann, "Prophecy and Fulfillment," in Westermann, ed., *Essays on Old Testament Hermeneutics*, 59.

39. Ibid., 72.

40. Ibid., 73.

41. I do not suggest that Jesus' message was confined to or defined by the promised land.

42. See the comments by Migliore, ed., in *The Church and Israel: Romans 9–11*, 4.

43. Here I am obviously thinking as a twentieth-century biblical scholar. The authors of the New Testament documents do not share our concern for the original meaning of a text. This observation acutely raises the issue of how the earliest Christians can help us in determining the relations between the Old and New Testaments. It is clear that we cannot assume that they have left no task for us to perform.

44. See the important comments by Roland E. Murphy and other leading OT specialists (e.g., James Barr and Joseph Blenkinsopp) on Child's position in the *Journal for the Study of the Old Testament* 16 (1980).

45. Three reliable reference works on the formation of the New Testament canon are the following: Roger Beckwith, *The Old Testament Canon of the New Testament Church and Its Background in Early Judaism* (Grand Rapids: Wm. B. Eerdmans, 1985); Brevard S. Childs, *The New Testament as Canon: An Introduction* (Philadelphia, Fortress Press: 1984); and William Farmer and Denis M. Farkasfalvy, *The Formation of the New Testament Canon* (Theological Inquiries; New York, Paulist Press: 1983).

46. James A. Sanders, *Torah and Canon* (Philadelphia: Fortress Press, 1972), x.

47. J. A. Sanders, *Torah and Canon*, xiv.

48. The New Testament authors apparently quoted from (or alluded to the inspired or authoritative nature of) the Ascension of Isaiah (Heb. 11:37), Testament of Moses (Jude 9), Baruch (1 Cor. 10:20; Rev. 8:2), 1 Enoch (Luke 16:9, 21:28; John 5:22; Col. 2:3; Heb. 11:5; 1 Pet. 1:12; Jude 14–15; Rev. 5:11, 15:3, 17:14, 19:16), 3 Maccabees (1 Tim. 6:15; Rev. 14:10, 17:14, 19:16, 20:10, 21:8), 4 Maccabees (Matt. 22:32; Rom. 7:7), Psalms of Solomon (Matt. 6:26; Luke 11:21–22; John 1:14; Rev. 2:26–27, 21:24, 26), many documents in the Old Testament Apocrypha, Aratus's *Phaenomena* 5 (Acts 17:28), Cleanthes (Acts 17:28), Epimenides *de Oraculis* (Titus 1:12), and Menander's *Thais* (1 Cor. 15:33).

49. See my discussion in *The Old Testament Pseudepigrapha and the New Testament* (SNTS Monograph Series 54; Cambridge: Cambridge University Press, 1985, 1987, 1988), 72–74. For the facsimile, see J. T. Milik, with M. Black, *The Books of Enoch:*

Aramaic Fragments from Qumran Cave 4 (Oxford: Clarendon Press, 1976), pl. 9.

50. Samuel Terrien, *The Elusive Presence: Toward a New Biblical Theology* (New York: San Francisco: Harper 1978), 470.

51. Ibid., 470.

52. Ibid., 472.

53. Ibid., 473.

54. Samuel E. Balentine, *The Hidden God: The Hiding of the Face of God in the Old Testament* (Oxford: Oxford University Press, 1983).

55. Terrien warns us to avoid the Latin rendering, which uses a passive participle, and to draw close to the original Hebrew, which employs the verbal reflexive. The translation is his; see Terrien, *The Elusive Presence*, 474.

56. Ibid., 475–476.

57. See B. A. Levine, "On the Presence of God in Biblical Religion," in *Religions in Antiquity: Essays in Memory of Erwin Ramsdell Goodenough*, ed. Jacob Neusner (SHR 14; Leiden, Neth.: E. J. Brill, 1968), 71–87.

58. See esp. 3 Baruch.

59. As Bultmann stated, "God is therefore unknowable for science." Bultmann, "Die Unerkennbarkeit Gottes," *Theologische Enzyklopädie*, ed. Eberhard Jüngel and Klaus W. Müller (Tübingen: J. C. B. Mohr, 1984), 51–59, esp. 51.

60. Bultmann does mention the Testament of Moses (which he called, following the customary practice at that time, the Assumption of Moses), 2 Baruch, and the Qaddish; but he did so to show that the apocalyptic writers dreamed of the dawning of God's kingdom. See Westermann, ed., *Essays on Old Testament Hermeneutics*, 65. He did not grasp the importance of these Jewish writings for helping to relate the two Testaments.

61. I think we may use this term with caution as we attempt to discern the relation of the Testaments. As I have argued in *The Old Testament Pseudepigrapha and the New Testament*, the term *intertestamental* can be very misleading; it offends those who have only the Hebrew Scriptures. It covers writings like 1 Enoch that antedate Daniel, and 4 Ezra, 2 Baruch, and many other writings that postdate 1 Thessalonians.

62. Edward Schillebeeckx, *Jesus: An Experiment in Christology*, trans. Hubert Hoskins (New York: Seabury Press 1979), 257.

63. See Migliore, ed., *The Church and Israel: Romans 9–11*.

64. The papers are published together in ibid.

65. See Miller, "Israelite Religion," in Knight and Tucker, eds., *The Hebrew Bible and Its Modern Interpreters*, 205.

66. For full documentation and discussion on the points made in the preceding sentences, see the proceedings of the first Princeton Symposium on Judaism and Christian Origins. See James H. Charlesworth, with J. Brownson, M. T. Davis, S. J. Kraftchick, and A. F. Segal, eds., *The Messiah:* Developments in Earliest Judaism and Christianity (Minneapolis: Fortress Press, 1992)

67. See the discussion of the various messianic ideas in the Dead Sea Scrolls by Lawrence Schiffman in Charlesworth et al., eds., *The Messiah*.

68. For text, translation, and discussion, see Joseph A. Fitzmyer, "The Contribution of Qumran Aramaic to the Study of the New Testament," *New Testament Studies* 20 (1974): 382–407.

69. Rudolf Bultmann, *Essays: Philosophical and Theological,* trans. J. C. G. Greig (London: 1955), 279. Bultmann contended that although the title "Son of God" "originally denoted the messianic king, [it] now takes on a new meaning which was self-evident to Gentile hearers. Now it comes to mean *the divinity of Christ, his divine nature.*" Bultmann, *Theology of the New Testament,* trans. Kendrick Grobel (New York: 1951), 1:128 [italics his]. For the most recent edition, see Bultmann, *Theologie des Neuen Testaments* (Uni-Taschenbücher 630; Tübingen: 1984), 131.

70. J. D. G. Dunn points out that it is "becoming increasingly probable that *the Son of God language of early Christianity has its roots with Jesus' own ministry.*" He goes on to point out that some fragments among the Dead Sea Scrolls (esp. 4QPs Dan A) demonstrate for the first time that "Son of God" had messianic significance in the Jewish theology of Jesus' day. Dunn, *Unity and Diversity in the New Testament* (Philadelphia: Trinity Press, 1990), 45.

71. Leonhard Goppelt, *Theology of the New Testament,* 2 vols., ed. J. Roloff, trans. John E. Alsup (Grand Rapids: Wm. B. Eerdmans, 1975, 1976); *Theologie des Neuen Testaments,* ed. Jürgen Roloff (Uni-Taschenbücher 850; Göttingen: Vandenhoeck & Ruprecht, 1985³). Martin Hengel, *The Son of God: The Origin of Christology and the History of Jewish-Hellenistic Religion,* trans. John Bowden (London, Philadelphia: Fortress Press, 1976 1967). C. F. D. Moule, *The Origin of Christology* (New York, Cambridge University Press: 1978). Ernst Käsemann, *New Testament Questions of Today* (New Testament Library; London: 1969), 37–38. I. Howard Marshall, *The Origins of New Testament Christology* (Issues in Contemporary Theology; Leicester, Eng.: Leicester University Press, 1976). Willi Marxsen, *The Beginnings*

of Christology, trans. Paul J. Achtemeier and Lorenz Nieting (Philadelphia: Fortress Press 1979). James H. Charlesworth, "The Jewish Roots of Christology and the Discovery of the Hypostatic Voice," *Scottish Journal of Theology* 39 (1986): 19–41; *Jesus Within Judaism: New Light from Exciting Archaeological Discoveries* (Anchor Bible Reference Library 1; New York: Doubleday, 1988).

72. See James H. Charlesworth, "From Jewish Messianology to Christian Christology: Some Caveats and Perspectives," in *Judaisms and Their Messiahs at the Turn of the Christian Era*, ed. J. Neusner et al. (New York: Cambridge University Press: 1987), 225–264.

73. For a lucid and informative account, see Robert J. Daly, *The Origins of the Christian Doctrine of Sacrifice* (Philadelphia: Fortress Press, 1978).

74. As M. Wilcox argued, the starting point of New Testament theology is not the proclamation (kerygma); it was the "common ground between Jew and Christian. But this does not mean merely the Old Testament, but rather the Old Testament understood in the light of the then accepted exegetical traditions." Wilcox, *Text and Interpretation: Studies in the New Testament Presented to Matthew Black*, ed. Ernest Best and R. M. Wilson (Cambridge: Cambridge University Press, 1979), 231–250.

75. Hebrew *abd* means only "servant."

76. Charlesworth, *Jesus Within Judaism.*

77. See James C. VanderKam "Righteous One, Messiah, Chosen One, and Son of Man in 1 Enoch 37–71" in Charlesworth et al., eds., *The Messiah*, 169–91.

78. E. E. Ellis argues that the New Testament authors' perspective for interpreting the Old Testament was "derived in part from contemporary Jewish views and in part from the teaching of Jesus and the experience of the reality of his resurrection." Ellis, *Prophecy and Hermeneutic in Early Christianity: New Testament Essays* (WUNT 18; Tübingen: 1978), 163.

79. See Joseph Heinemann, *Prayer in the Talmud: Forms and Patterns* (Studia Judaica 9; Berlin, New York: de Gruyter 1977).

80. Ernst Käsemann, "On the Subject of Primitive Christian Apocalyptic," in *New Testament Questions of Today* trans. W. J. Montague (London: SCM Press 1969), 108–137.

81. J. Christiaan Beker, *Paul the Apostle* (Philadelphia: Fortress Press 1980); Martinus de Boer, *The Defeat of Death: Apocalyptic Eschatology in 1 Corinthians 15 and Romans 5* (*Journal for the Study of the New Testament*, Supplement Series 22; Sheffield, Eng.: JSOT Press 1988).

82. Bultmann, "Prophecy and Fulfillment," in Westermann, ed., *Essays on Old Testament Hermeneutics*, 52–55.

83. Surely, we professors can no longer allow the interpretation of Isaiah 7 that does violence to the original meaning of the Hebrew and becomes simply a proof of Jesus' virginal birth. At the same time, we must attempt to refine historical criticism, which has violated the intention of the biblical authors and thrust their texts deep into the past so that their message as originally intended is rendered silent. See the major attempts to improve the presuppositions and use of historical criticism by F. Hahn and Peter Stuhlmacher. Ferdinand Hahn, *Historical Investigation and New Testament Faith*, trans. Robert Maddox (Philadelphia: Fortress Press, 1983); and Peter Stuhlmacher, *Historical Criticism and Theological Interpretation of Scripture*, trans. Ray A. Harrisville (Philadelphia: Fortress Press 1977). Also see Martin Hengel, *Zur urchristlichen Geschichtsschreibung* ET, *Earliest Christianity*, trans. *Acts and the History of Earliest Christianity*, John Bowden (London: SCM, 1986) (Philadelphia, Fortress Press 1980) (Stuttgart: Calwev Verlag 1984). The supersessionist interpretation of the OT can no longer be tolerated. See esp. Roger Brooks and John J. Collins, eds., *Hebrew Bible or Old Testament: Studying the Bible in Judaism and Christianity* (Notre Dame, Ind., University of Notre Dame Press, 1990).

84. This term, *save*, is not a Christian concept as many, including Jewish scholars, have implied. It is a term found in the Old Testament and is abundant in the intertestamental literature. An examination of *g'l* (meaning "to redeem") and its cognates, and *yshc* (Ni, "to be saved") and its cognates in the Hebrew of the Old Testament, in the Dead Sea Scrolls, and in the Mishnah reveals how important "salvation" and "redemption" is in the history of the theology of Israel and Judaism.

85. The latter prophets did look to the future and did "foretell"; but the prophets were not primarily foretellers. They served their contemporaries' present needs and stood within the perspective that Yahweh would redeem the people through history (*Heilsgeschichte*).

86. See the informative reflections on the seminal use of 1 Enoch in the formation of the kerygma by Matthew Black, "The Theological Appropriation of the Old Testament by the New Testament," *Scottish Journal of Theology* 39 (1986): 1–17.

87. I am aware that this dimension of the Bible has been pointed out many times, but it needs reemphasis.

88. James H. Charlesworth, ed., *Jesus' Jewishness: Exploring the Place of Jesus within Early Judaism* (New York: Crossroad, 1991).

89. Contrast the positions of both Bultmann and Friedrich Baumgartel, but see the insightful and sensitive criticism of their positions by Eichrodt in "Is Typological Exegesis an Appropriate Method?" in Westermann, ed., *Essays on Old Testament Hermeneutics*, 224–245.

90. See the articles by von Rad and Eichrodt in Westermann, ed., *Essays on Old Testament Hermeneutics*.

91. See the helpful chart and discussion by George W. Buchanan, *Typology and the Gospel* (New York, London: University Press of America 1987).

92. Leonhard Goppelt focused attention early in his career on the concept of typology. His *Theology of the New Testament* contains numerous examples of how he employs typology (see the index, "typology" in vol. 2, p. 348). In some examples I am not persuaded that he has corrected the concept of salvation history and time, which was a presupposition for the repetition that undergirded typological exegesis in antiquity. Typology must be used with careful controls and a refined perception of the relation of the Testaments. It should be employed at the end of a detailed examination of how the New Testament is related to the Old.

93. Paul D. Hanson, *The People Called: The Growth of Community in the Bible* (San Francisco: Harper & Row, 1986, 1988), 386.

94. Biblical theologians have recognized this aspect of the Bible, but it needs to be more widely appreciated.

95. James Barr, *Old and New in Interpretation: A Study of the Two Testaments* (London: SCM Press 1966).

96. See the insights shared by W. D. Davies in "Reflections About the Use of the Old Testament in the New in Its Historical Context," *Jewish Quarterly Review* 74 (1983): 105–136. Also, one of the best, most thorough discussions of the use of the Old in the New is by D. M. Smith in his "The Use of the Old Testament in the New," in *The Use of the Old Testament in the New and Other Essays: Studies in Honor of William Franklin Stinespring*, ed. James M. Efird (Durham, N.C.: Duke University Press, 1972), 3–65.

97. See the fruitful suggestions by Donald Juel in *Messianic Exegesis: Christological Interpretation of the Old Testament in Early Christianity* (Philadelphia: 1988).

98. Similar thoughts were published by Zimmerli in 1952. Note this challenge: "If Christ is to be understood in the way which we have indicated, in his proper nature as the fulfillment of the promise to Israel, then a certain conversation is unavoid-

able: the conversation with the historical Israel." Zimmerli, in Westermann, ed., *Essays on Old Testament Hermeneutics*, 121.

99. See the numerous studies in *Mikra: Text, Translation, Reading and Interpretation of the Hebrew Bible in Ancient Judaism and Early Christianity*, ed. Martin J. Mulder and Harry Sysling (Compendia Rerum Iudaicarum ad Novum Testamentum 2.1; Assen/Maastricht, Philadelphia: Fortress Press 1988).

100. Moshe Weinfeld, "The Day of the Lord: Aspirations for the Kingdom of God in the Bible and Jewish Liturgy," in *Studies in Bible*, ed. Sara Japhet (Scripta Hierosolymitana 31; Jerusalem: Magnes Press, Hebrew University 1986), 341–372; the quotation is on pp. 371–372.

101. Quoted in the fourth century c.e. by Shenoute, Abbot of Athribis in Egypt. See E. Amélineau, *Oeuvres de Schenoudi* (Paris: 1914), 2:379–380. I am grateful to Professor Moshe Weinfeld, who learned about this important passage from Professor A. Shisha-Halevy of the Hebrew University in Jerusalem.

102. R. J. Zwi Werblowsky, "Faith, Hope and Trust: A Study of Bittahon," *Papers of the Institute of Jewish Studies London*, ed. J. G. Weiss (Jerusalem: 1964), 95–139. The quotation is on p. 104.

103. See Paul Ricoeur, "History and Hermeneutics," in *Philosophy of History and Action*, ed. Yirmiahu Yovel (Jerusalem: 1978), 3–20. Also Boston: D. Reidel Pub. Co., 1978.

104. H. B. Swete found Old Testament allusions in 278 of the 404 verses in Revelation. Swete, *The Apocalypse of St. John* (London: 1911), cxl. D. M. Smith concludes (with J. A. Montgomery) that the author of Revelation derives his Old Testament allusions from "the rich storehouse of" his own memory. Smith, "The Use of the Old Testament in the New," in Efird, ed., *The Use of the Old Testament in the New and Other Essays*, 61.

105. Melanchthon's *Loci communes rerum theologicarum* were intended to lead Christians to the Scriptures. They however led to proof texts that treated the Bible superficially. See the insightful critique by John H. Hayes and Frederick Prussner, *Old Testament Theology: Its History and Development* (Atlanta: John Knox Press 1985), 15–19. See George W. Coats's criticism of constructing a theology of the Old Testament according to criteria derived from Christian systematic theology. Coats, "Theology of the Hebrew Bible," Knight and Tucker, eds., *The Hebrew Bible and Its Modern Interpreters*, 239–262.

106. In addition to the collection of essays on the relation of the Testaments edited by Bernhard W. Anderson and Claus Westermann and already noted, see *The Relationship Between the Old and New Testament* (Neotestamentica 14; Bloemfontein, South Africa: Bloemfontein, South Africa: NTSSA, 1981).

3

Apocalypticism as a Bridge Between the Testaments

John J. Carey

There are various ways by which one can probe the theme of the relationship between the Old and New Testaments. That theme, although broad, is complex and subtle. It has historical, social, and theological dimensions. Much scholarly work has been done in this area. We are certainly indebted to the work of giants such as Bernhard W. Anderson, W. D. Davies, Frederick C. Grant, Martin Hengel, Millar Burrows, Henry Cadbury, Walther Eichrodt, and Gerhard von Rad. We could, following Eichrodt's lead, pursue the theological theme of the covenant as a link between the Testaments.[1] Or we could, following the important work of James Charlesworth, probe the richness of the intertestamental literature.[2] Recent work on popular movements within the Judaism of Jesus' time suggests still a third rich option.[3] We could fruitfully compare some of the newer sociological analyses that have studied the social context of ancient Israel and of the early church,[4] and much of the recent work on Jesus has underscored the importance of seeing him within his Jewish matrix.[5] We are not lacking for suggestions, nor for roads already developed and traveled.

Apocalypticism as a Bridge
Between the Testaments

After a good bit of reflection, and with some incentive provided by Elisabeth Schüssler Fiorenza's excellent analysis of the book of Revelation entitled *The Book of Revelation: Justice and Judgment*,[6] I decided to go in a different direction and explore the theme of apocalypticism as a bridge between the Testaments. I chose this theme with some trepidation; as a teacher, I have found the classic Old Testament apocalyptic passages in Isaiah 56–66 (so-called Third Isaiah), Zechariah 12–14, and Daniel 7–12 mysterious and complicated. Other passages—such as Isaiah 24–27, Joel 2:28—3:31, and most of the Book of Malachi, filled as they are with visions of a fallen world, judgment by Yahweh, and the elimination of sorrow and death—seemed to fall into a poetic category appropriate to the aspirations of ancient Israel, and to have limited contemporary significance. I was mindful, of course, that various New Testament writers drew on this Hebrew heritage of visions of the end time, and all the Gospel writers were clearly influenced by the categories of Jewish apocalypticism. In Matthew 24, just to cite one example, Jesus cautions that before that very generation would pass away,

> the sun will be darkened,
> and the moon will not give its light;
> the stars will fall from heaven,
> and the powers of heaven will be shaken. . . .

> All the tribes of the earth will mourn, and they will see the Son of Man coming on the clouds of heaven with power and great glory. And he will send out his angels with a loud trumpet call, and they will gather his elect from the four winds, from one end of heaven to the other. (vv. 29–31)[7]

Other well-known examples of this urgent sense of the end time are found in Mark 13; in 1 Thessalonians 4, where Paul says that at the end time the dead in Christ will rise first; then those who are alive will meet the Lord Jesus in midair; in 2 Thessalonians 2, where Paul describes the reign of the anti-Christ, which will precede the coming of the Lord Jesus; Hebrews 12:18–29; 1 Peter 4; and, of course, almost the entire Book of Revelation. All of these passages are well known, and we do not have to belabor the point that apocalyptic visions and language link the world of early Christianity with its Jewish ancestors. It is important to clarify at the outset, however, that the terms *apocalyptic* and *apocalypticism* can refer to a genre of literature or to a mind-set. The visions of Daniel and the Apocalypse of John are examples of apocalyptic literature; the examples that Paul uses about meeting the Lord in midair and the appearance of the anti-Christ are examples of a mind-set—a way of thinking.

Although a working premise in this essay is that apocalyptic thinking is one of the basic links between the Old and New Testaments, it needs to be stressed that the use of apocalyptic imagery was not confined to ancient Judaism and to early Christianity. Other faiths and cultures also depicted their expectation of the end time with visions, battles, cosmic struggles, justice, and judgment.[8] What the Jews adapted as their own apparently had earlier roots in Persian, Egyptian, and Oriental cultures. Dramatic, vivid depictions of the end time, complete with destruction, judgment, renewal, and reward, were a part of the ancient *zeitgeist*. It is beyond the scope of this essay to discuss in detail the roots of Hebraic apocalyptic thinking; suffice it to say that most scholars see some ties to the movement of Hebrew prophecy, with its calls for righteousness, judgment, and the ultimate vindication of Yahweh. There is surely a second impetus in the political defeats of both Israel and Judah, and in the pain and persecutions related to those experiences. Much of Hebrew messianism and the "Son of Man" tradition is related to these same events. That history, as well as those thought categories, was inherited by the writers of the New Testament.

The New Testament Impact
on Apocalyptic Thinking

A critical theological question, of course, is whether or not the New Testament writers change the focus and intent of the Old Testament apocalyptic language. Clearly, most of Old Testament apocalypticism was related to the belief in God as Creator, to the promises of God, the judgment of God, and the restoration of the righteous ones of Israel. It mirrors the yearnings of a small community for restoration. There is some evidence of universalism in the Gospels (note the parable of the Great Dinner in Luke 14:15–24), so that we could say that in at least one stream of the New Testament the sense of the "righteous community" is much broader than it was in the Old Testament. In spite of the Gentile mission, in the post-Pauline period the apocalyptic categories of early Christianity apply again to a small group—persecuted, misunderstood, suffering, and struggling for its life. Although the community changes and the theological referents change, I believe that the categories of apocalyptic thought and the intention of apocalyptic thinking remain the same. I believe it is legitimate, therefore, to speak of biblical apocalypticism and to see this genre of thought as a major link between the Testaments.

Interpretations of Apocalypticism

Not many of us are biblical literalists, and not many of us, if pressed, would say that we expect to meet the Lord Jesus in midair; nor do we expect to see the Lord Jesus slay the son of perdition with the breath of his mouth (2 Thess. 2:8). George Frideric Handel notwithstanding, we do not expect to be alerted to the last day with the pealing of trumpets. What then can we say about this kind of language, these kinds of visions, these dreams and yearnings for a better day and better world? Do visions of the archangel Gabriel, beasts with horns, horsemen of the apocalypse, and bloody battles of the sons of light against the sons of darkness have any relevance for us today? Or are they the quaint expressions of the prescientific mind and the quixotic yearnings of ancient peoples?

Many modern interpreters, including Paul S. Minear, John J. Collins, and Paul D. Hanson, have argued for the ongoing relevance of the biblical apocalyptic message, stressing that the biblical language is symbolic, insightful, broad in its grasp of ultimate human realities, and profound in its meaning for people of faith.[9] With these emphases they support the earlier contentions of Amos Wilder, George B. Caird, and H. H. Rowley.[10] Paul D. Hanson, whose work on apocalypticism has been at the forefront of the contemporary discussion, has stressed that apocalypticism in both the Old and New Testaments mirrors the attempt to understand some of the most troubling aspects of life: conflict between nations, moral paradoxes, the suffering of the innocent, martyrdom, and the failure of divine promises to come to fulfillment.[11] He further points out that this type of writing—this yearning for a better day and for the reward of the righteous—tends to come from, and speak to, those who are on the fringes of society: political prisoners, hunted dissidents, and those who struggle daily to find sufficient food and water to sustain life.[12] Indeed, with the right hermeneutic, these strange, bizarre descriptions of ancient writers can remind us that, then and now, the world looks different to dispossessed and marginal people than it looks to the privileged and comfortable, who assume that their place in the structure of things is divinely ordained (This distinction is one of the major themes of Liberation Theology.) We forget that lesson at our own peril.

Apocalypticism and Early Christianity

Let us turn now to consider not only how apocalypticism linked the Testaments but how it shaped the whole consciousness of early Christianity. It was in 1960 that Ernst Käsemann, the distinguished pupil of Rudolf Bultmann and subsequent professor at Tübingen, published an essay that later appeared in English as "The Beginnings of Christian Theology."[13] In that essay he argued that "apocalyptic was the mother of all Christian theology." The essay, like so many of Käsemann's other essays, aroused a good bit of controversy, and he wrote a subsequent essay entitled "On the Subject of Primitive Christian Apocalyptic," which defended and clarified his position.

Actually, Käsemann's argument shows some affinities with, as well as differences from, the older viewpoint of the "thoroughgoing eschatology" associated with Albert Schweitzer, Johannes Weiss, and Martin Werner.[14] Käsemann defined primitive Christian apocalypticism as "the expectation of an imminent Parousia" and was especially interested in clues in Matthew's Gospel that point to that expectation. (I stress that to clarify that Käsemann, in this essay at least, was not particularly interested in Paul's use of apocalyptic language nor in the symbols or categories of the Book of Revelation.) Early Christianity, Käsemann argued, was born with the fervent expectation of the return of Jesus, who sits in the interim on the throne as the Son of Man, as a sign of the triumph of the righteousness of God. This was itself a shift from the message of Jesus, which Käsemann interprets as focusing on the service of God, the love of our neighbors and our enemies, and the omnipresent grace and mercy of God. So Jesus was nonapocalyptic, in Käsemann's view;[15] but the early church cast its whole message in apocalyptic categories, and in that sense "apocalypticism was the mother of Christian theology." Although this hope proved to be a delusion, Käsemann felt that such a hope is still critical to Christian proclamation. He muses:

We have to ask ourselves whether Christian theology can ever survive in any legitimate form without this theme, which sprang from the Easter experience and determined the Easter faith.[16]

I have a broader goal in this essay than just analyzing Käsemann's argument, but I cite it to demonstrate that when we reflect on the meaning of apocalyptic visions, the nature of apocalyptic language, and the power of apocalyptic thought, we are not dealing with a tangential feature of the Christian tradition. When someone of Ernst Käsemann's stature calls apocalypticism "the mother of all Christian theology," we need to take note of this phenomenon. Any serious student of apocalypticism has to struggle with the question raised by Schubert Ogden over twenty-five years ago; that is, whether it is possible to speak of Christ without myth—and if so, what is the style and substance of such a proclamation?[17] I will bracket for our purposes the various criticisms directed at Käsemann, such as his tendency to offer a very limited definition of what apocalypticism is (he basically equates it with the eschatological expectation of the Parousia), his conviction that the teaching of Jesus was not basically shaped by apocalyptic motifs, and the counterclaim of his opponents that the earliest preaching in Acts centers more on the resurrection than on the Parousia.[18] The issue of apocalypticism is so important that it does not matter if Käsemann's interpretation of it needs revising. It is not surprising, therefore, that images of the Second Coming and final judgment have been depicted vividly in art, poetry, and in novels,[19] and many theologians maintain that it is the basis of all Christian hope.

The Continuing Significance of Apocalypticism

The larger issue, of course, is what we should do today with the biblical categories of apocalypticism. At one level such language is primitive, outdated, and

embarrassing, yet all pastors know that this figurative
and symbolic language is still a source of comfort to people in times of grief and stress. Even demythologized, it
points us to hope, assurance, and the power of God. So
pastorally one could argue that we need to keep this terminology for use in sermons, counseling, and funeral
meditations. What pastor has not used, in times of grief,
the great poetic reassurances of the Book of Revelation?

For this reason they are before the throne of God,
 and serve him day and night within his temple,
 and the one who is seated on the throne will shelter them.
They will hunger no more, and thirst no more;
 the sun will not strike them,
 nor any scorching heat;
for the Lamb at the center of the throne will be their shepherd,
 and he will guide them to springs of the water of life,
and God will wipe away every tear from their eyes. (7:15–17)

At a practical and political level, the language of
apocalypticism also has contemporary relevance. The various predictions of economists, social scientists, and ecol-
ogists about the exhaustion of the resources of our planet,
the consequences of the virtual rape of the earth by cor-
porate interests, and the virtual enslavement of the have-
nots of the world by the driving economic needs of the
First World, have all reminded us of the fragile nature of
life, of human exploitation and greed, and of the precari-
ous nature of our quality of life. Suddenly, the apocalyptic visions of doom, judgment, and wrath have a cogency
and relevancy that in our more optimistic moments we
had been inclined to overlook. So even if we do not think
much these days about the Son of Man seated on the
throne of glory, or of meeting Jesus in midair, or about
God's master plan as rewarding the righteous, we think a
lot about the four horsemen of the apocalypse, and of
plagues, pestilence, and destruction. The grim side of
apocalypticism is still with us, and both theologically and
politically it still informs Christian thought.

A Darker Side to Apocalyptic Thinking

In these two previous characteristics, I have noted some of the positive and relevant aspects of apocalypticism. But it also has a negative, dark, or problematic side. In almost all of its forms, apocalyptic thinking is based upon and fosters a sharp dualism: a contrast between two ages, with a sharp break between them; pessimism toward the present age and hope for a world to come; judgment on God's enemies and salvation for God's people; a keen sense of who are the sons of darkness and of who are the sons of light. Apocalypticism pivots on the difference between good and evil, purity and impurity, the powerful and the helpless, the holy and the profane. As such, for traditions like Christendom, which inherit, breathe, and use those categories, it fosters mentalities of exclusivism: of "us" and "them," of "insiders and outsiders," of the people of God struggling in a large, hostile, and pagan world. Dualism fosters a nation of exclusivity. It reminds us that unknown people, or different cultures, are "other" than we are. It isolates the stranger, for in dualistic thought all others are either with us or against us. Apocalyptic thinking from Daniel to Revelation did tighten the bonds of the community of faith, but it did so at a terrible price: it hardens the religious community against the outsider. Surely, the ancient Hebraic concepts of purity need to be seen in this context, and the early Christian tensions between Jews and Gentiles mirror that as well. Most of the exclusive Christian theological claims to truth, most of the Christian postures that look down on other religions, and most of the claims that Christianity is qualitatively different from all other religious faiths are rooted in this model of dualistic thinking. Assumptions of Christian exclusivism have reigned among sectarian groups and have dominated conservative groups within the Christian family, and they are still found within mainline bodies. That kind of thinking has a hard time with religious and cultural pluralism, and in that regard may be leading us backward rather than forward as we approach the third millennium.

Getting Beyond Exclusivism

My basic contention is that the modern church needs to go beyond the exclusivism associated with apocalypticism. Yes, we need to study the roots of that mode of thought in ancient Israel and in other cultures. Yes, we need to acknowledge that the symbols, imagery, visions, and dreams of ancient writers entered directly into the bloodstream and consciousness of the early Christian community: Jesus, Paul, and the authors of Hebrews and the Revelation of John. Yes, Käsemann may have been right to call apocalypticism "the mother of all Christian theology." Yes, there are insights in apocalyptic terminology that are pastorally and politically helpful for the Christian ministry today. But the very foundations of this way of thinking fail us where we all need help today— that is, how we as Christians can relate to other faiths, traditions, peoples, and cultures.

Most of us recognize how the world has changed in our lifetimes. Both communications and world events have forced all of us into a broader global awareness. Terms such as "the Third World," "Central America," "the former Soviet Union," "the Pacific Rim," "emerging industrial nations" now shape our political and social consciousness. The fundamentalists of Islam and the priests of Buddhism have crowded into our national and personal consciousness as uninvited guests. We have learned, often to our great pain and embarrassment, that not only nations but also cultures and religions clash. Parochialism is a luxury that we can no longer afford. So the encounter of Christianity with the other great world religions presents us with a new theological agenda. Even Paul Tillich, to whom so many of us owe so much, saw this coming in the last few years of his life and devoted his Chicago years (1962–65) to exploring the methods and possibilities of a comparative study of Christianity and other world religions.[20] Tillich noted at the end of his life that if he were able to live his life over again he would not have confined his interests so narrowly to the West, but would have turned much earlier to Eastern cultures and religions.

A new body of literature has emerged in the last few years that mirrors this engagement, and many conferences have been held to further this dialogue.[21] I cannot begin to survey this literature, but I do believe that a "paradigm shift" has occurred in our theological consciousness and that substantial new perspectives have grown out of the theological engagements of Christianity with Islam, Buddhism, Hinduism, and Judaism. Some of the key contributors to this new theological viewpoint have been John Cobb, Wilfred Cantwell Smith, Raimundo Panikkar, Tom S. Driver, Leonard Swidler, and Hans Küng. Orbis Press, the Center for the Study of World Religions at Harvard, the East-West Center at the University of Hawaii, the Claremont School of Theology, and the *Journal of Ecumenical Studies* at Temple University have all played major roles in bringing this dialogue into print. Key intellectual factors in this broad attempt to "deabsolutize" truth claims have been (1) our historical knowledge that dogmatic claims are contextual, relative, and relational; (2) the insights from the sociology of knowledge (developed originally by Karl Mannheim and popularized in this country by Peter Berger and Thomas Luckmann); (3) our awareness (from Wittgenstein and others) of the limitations of all language; and (4) the work done on hermeneutics, especially by Hans-Georg Gadamer and Paul Ricoeur, which has reminded us that all knowledge is interpreted knowledge.[22] I realize that in the world of ministry these names and currents may seem a bit esoteric, but in the world of scholars I think it is fair to say that few persons anymore defend the notion of pure truth, pure dogma, or infallible claims. Theologically, that has opened channels for listening, comparing, learning, and bridge building.

Hans Küng, to whom I personally owe so much, is a case in point. I spent a sabbatical with Küng at his Ecumenical Institute at the University of Tübingen, and I was first drawn to him when he electrified the Christian world by insisting that the Second Vatican Council face the issue of reconciliation with the Protestants. His concern for ecumenical matters has, of course, seriously strained his relations with the Vatican and with conservative Catholics, but his theological pilgrimmage can serve as a paradigm for this new shift of consciousness that I am describing. Küng has taken seriously the task of opening a dialogue with other faiths. He coauthored a major work dealing with Christianity's engagement with Islam, Hinduism, and Buddhism.[23] He has boldly sketched out the shape and agenda of an ecumenical theology of the future, entitled *A Theology for the Third Millennium.*[24] In a recent essay entitled "What Is True Religion? Toward an Ecumenical Criteriology," Küng argues that a norm of authentic humanness should be the benchmark by which we assess currents of our own tradition and of other traditions. He writes:

> Insofar as a religion serves humanness, insofar as in its creedal and moral doctrines, its rites and institutions, it *fosters* human beings in their human identity, meaningfulness, and value, and helps them gain a meaningful and fruitful existence, it is a *true* and *good* religion.
>
> Insofar as a religion spreads inhumaneness, insofar as in its creedal and moral doctrines, its rites and institutions, it hinders human beings in their human identity, meaningfulness, and value, and thus helps them fail to gain a meaningful and fruitful existence, it is a *false* and *bad* religion.[25]

In every major religious tradition—Christianity, Buddhism, Hinduism, Islam, and Judaism—one can find examples of both good and evil, truth and untruth. All of these traditions have their prophets, reformers, sages, and saints. No tradition is pure, nor qualitatively different from others. So Küng reminds us that the theological mind-set of the future is not one that dualistically sets itself against all others; rather, it is a viewpoint that can make discriminating judgments about what enhances humanity in all religious faiths.

This broader, more humanistic perspective does not require detachment from the community of faith, nor is it inconsistent with a "high" Christology that sees Jesus as one through whom God has acted to convey a revelation to all peoples. A servant Christology and a LOGOS Christology are readily adapted to this viewpoint, as both Raimundo Pannikar and John Cobb have shown.[26] Most scholars agree that the truth of any religion can be known only "from within," as a practicing member of that tradition. One can say with intensity, therefore, that Christianity is the true faith *for me*; because its history, heritage, symbols, and faith claims have shaped me, molded me, and given me a perspective on life's meaning and its end. That claim, in global theology, does not deny the power or validity of other faiths; it can even acknowledge that other faiths possess truths that we have only implicitly.

And what, we might ask, does this new type of ecumenical thinking stand for? Again following Küng's lead, we can mention:

1. It repudiates all religious wars, persecutions, and inquisitions, and affirms respect of all persons, religious tolerance, and a solidarity of love among peoples.

2. It does not dwell on the sins and guilt of other traditions; it instead practices forgiveness and dares a new beginning.

3. It does not try to eliminate religious communities or institutions, but tries to relativize their claims for the welfare of humanity.

4. It tries to be a force for reconciliation among religious groups, cultures, and nations, and urges
peace among religious groups as a prerequisite for
peace among the nations.[27]

Conclusion

Let us now in summary double back to where we
began—the legacy of apocalyptic thought on our thinking
as Christian men and women. This way of viewing the
world, inspired by prophetic calls of judgment and the
reward of the righteous, shaped the mentality of the first
Christians just as a mother's milk gives life to an infant.
Those convictions, magnified by times of persecution,
caused much (if not all) of first-century Christianity to live
with the hope of the Parousia. In this essay I have tried
to point out our dialectical debt to this mode of thought.
It has simultaneously blessed us and cursed us. It has
conveyed across centuries the element of hope, and it has
spoken to theological, political, and moral paradoxes.
Even in a demythologized form it has reminded us of the
cries of the marginal and the oppressed. Time and again
the lords of economic and political power confirm the
biblical visions of the greed of the high and mighty.

Yet I have tried to clarify that the apocalyptic mind-
sets of the Old and New Testaments are products of a
narrower, more parochial way of looking at the world,
and the sharp dualism of apocalypticism limits us from
seeing, and coping with, a much broader global reality.
Apocalypticism has, on the whole, reinforced biblical lit-
eralism and strengthened the sense of Christian exclusivism. Although it nurtures the inner life, it is confusing as
to how it depicts the broader world. We have had enough
of Western theological imperialism, of religious intoler-
ance and fanaticism, and of leadership that divides. The
technological, economic, and political interpenetration of

cultures has preceded our efforts at interreligious under-standing, and I am persuaded that that task really is the theological agenda of the future.

So in the context of a rapidly changing world, I invite you to reconsider our apocalyptic heritage, to see its strengths and limitations—and to go beyond it.

Notes

1. Walther Eichrodt, *Theology of the Old Testament* (Philadel-phia: Westminster Press, 1961, 1967), 2 vols., passim. It is now generally acknowledged, however, that Eichrodt defined this covenant motif very broadly and virtually ignored other parts of the Old Testament that do not fit so neatly into the covenant theme.

2. See James H. Charlesworth, *The Old Testament Pseudepigrapha* (New York: Doubleday, 1983, 1985), 2 vols.

3. See Richard A. Horsley with John S. Hanson, *Bandits, Prophets, and Messiahs: Popular Movements at the Time of Jesus* (San Francisco: Harper & Row, 1986), and Horsley's *Jesus and the Spiral of Violence: Popular Jewish Resistance in Roman Palestine* (San Francisco: Harper & Row, 1987).

4. See Norman K. Gottwald's *The Hebrew Bible: A Socio-Literary Introduction* (Philadelphia: Fortress Press, 1985), esp. 26–34, as well as his "Sociological Method in the Study of Ancient Israel," in *Encounter with the Text*, ed. Martin J. Buss (Philadelphia: Fortress Press, 1979), 69–81, and his edited book, *The Bible and Liberation: Political and Social Hermeneutics* (Mary-knoll, N.Y.: Orbis Books, 1983). Cf. Howard C. Kee's *Christian Origins: A Sociological Perspective* (Philadelphia: Westminster Press, 1980), and Gerd Theissen's *Sociology of Early Palestinian Christianity* (Philadelphia: Fortress Press, 1977).

5. Two good examples of this trend are E. P. Sanders' *Jesus and Judaism* (Philadelphia: Fortress Press, 1985) and James H. Charlesworth's *Jesus Within Judaism: New Light from Exciting Archaeological Discoveries* (New York: Doubleday, 1988). Broader trends in Jesus research are analyzed by Charlesworth in his "From Barren Mazes to Gentle Rappings: The Emergence of Jesus Research," *Princeton Seminary Bulletin* 7 (1986): 221–230, and Marcus Borg's "A Renaissance in Jesus Studies," *Today* 45, no. 3 (October 1988): 280–292.

6. Elisabeth Schüssler Fiorenza, *The Book of Revelation: Jus-tice and Judgment* (Philadelphia: Fortress Press, 1985.) This book

is a collection of various studies that Schüssler Fiorenza has published on the Book of Revelation. It has an especially valuable Introduction on "Research Perspectives on the Book of Revelation," which reviews recent literature and clarifies the controversies surrounding the interpretation of that work. Although I am basically more interested in Schüssler Fiorenza's work in feminist biblical hermeneutics than I am in her various studies of the Book of Revelation, this book impressed me with its analysis of the importance of apocalyptic writing for early Christianity.

7. There is, of course, considerable question as to whether these words are authentically traceable to Jesus or whether they reflect the mentality and faith of Matthew. Bultmann and Käsemann both ascribe this vision to Matthew and not to Jesus.

8. The best collection of extrabiblical apocalyptic writings is Edgar Hennecke, ed., *New Testament Apocrypha* (Philadelphia: Westminster Press, 1965), vol. 2. The Old Testament roots of apocalyptic thought are treated in Paul D. Hanson, *The Dawn of Apocalyptic* (Philadelphia: Fortress Press, 1976).

9. See Paul S. Minear, *New Testament Apocalyptic* (Nashville: Abingdon Press, 1981); John J. Collins, *The Apocalyptic Imagination: An Introduction to the Jewish Matrix of Christianity* (New York: Crossroad, 1984); and the various writings of Hanson, including the one cited in note 8.

10. See H. H. Rowley's *The Relevance of Apocalyptic* (New York: Association Press, 1963); Amos Wilder's *Early Christian Rhetoric: The Language of the Gospel* (Cambridge: Harvard University Press, 1971); and George B. Caird's excellent commentary on the Book of Revelation entitled *The Revelation of St. John the Divine* (New York: Harper & Row, 1966).

11. Paul D. Hanson, *Old Testament Apocalyptic* (Nashville: Abingdon Press, 1987), 22.

12. Ibid.

13. Ernst Käsemann, "The Beginnings of Christian Theology," in *New Testament Questions of Today* (Naperville, Ill.: Alec R. Allenson, 1969), 82–107.

14. The classic work of this viewpoint was, of course, Schweitzer's *The Quest of the Historical Jesus* (New York: Macmillan, 1906, 1961).

15. On this point Käsemann differs from Albert Schweitzer, who saw Jesus as fully embracing the worldview of Jewish apocalypticism. Käsemann seems to enjoy the support of the recently formed "Jesus Seminar" in this dispute; see Borg, "A Renaissance in Jesus Studies," 285–287.

16. Käsemann, "The Beginnings of Christian Theology," 107.

17. See Shubert Ogden's *Christ Without Myth* (New York: Harper & Row, 1961).

18. A survey of the debate that Käsemann precipitated is found in I. Howard Marshall's article "Is Apocalyptic the Mother of Christian Theology?" in *Tradition and Interpretation in the New Testament*, ed. Gerald F. Hawthorne with Otto Betz (Grand Rapids: Wm. B. Eerdmans, 1988), 33–41.

19. Some illustrations of this would be Albrecht Dürer's woodcuts on *The Apocalypse* and John Milton's poetic depictions in *Paradise Lost*. John R. May analyzes the importance of the apocalyptic motif in American novels in his book *Toward a New Earth: Apocalypse in the American Novel* (Notre Dame, Ind.: University of Notre Dame Press, 1972).

20. See Paul Tillich's *Christianity and the Encounter with World Religions* (New York: Harper & Row, 1960) and the essays in *The Future of Religion* (New York: Harper & Row, 1967) that grew out of his seminars at Chicago with Mircea Eliade.

21. One major international meeting representative of this movement was held in Kyoto, Japan, in October of 1970. A declaration coming from that meeting is reprinted in Leonard Swidler's essay "Interreligious and Interideological Dialogue," in Leonard Swidler, ed., *Toward a Universal Theology of Religion* (Maryknoll, N.Y.: Orbis Books, 1987), 29–30.

22. For further elaboration of these points, see ibid., 7–10.

23. See Hans Küng, Josef van Ess, Heinrich von Stietencron, and Heinz Bechert, *Christianity and the World Religions: Paths to Dialogue with Islam, Hinduism, and Buddhism* (New York: Doubleday, 1986).

24. Hans Küng, *A Theology for the Third Millennium* (New York: Doubleday, 1988).

25. In Swidler, ed., *Toward a Universal Theology of Religion*, 242.

26. See Raimundo Pannikar's *The Unknown Christ of Hinduism* (Maryknoll, N.Y.: Orbis Press, 1981), and John Cobb's *Christ in a Pluralistic Age* (Philadelphia: Westminster Press, 1984).

27. In Swidler, ed., *Toward a Universal Theology of Religion*, 248.

4

Christ the Servant of the Lord

R. Frank Johnson

When we explore the relationship between the Old and New Testaments,[1] it is appropriate to examine the ways in which one particular text and its related theological themes have functioned within the Bible for first-century Judaism and for the early church and its writers. Certainly, few texts have exerted a more determinative influence on first-century Palestinian Judaism and on New Testament writers than the celebrated Servant Songs from Second Isaiah. Emerging from the very earliest stages of Christology, pre-Pauline and pre-Gospel traditions interpreted Jesus of Nazareth, both his life and mission, using motifs and images drawn from the servant passages. These early theologians understood Jesus as fulfilling the prophecies announced by Second Isaiah, and found in the servant the prototype (ideal or historical) of a humiliated-exalted servant chosen by God to bear the sins of all persons. More specifically, the Gospel writers are overtly conspicuous in their efforts to parallel Jesus with the servant. The fourth Servant Song in Isaiah 52:13ff. may well have served as a prototype for interpreting (and perhaps reconstructing) Jesus' life in the Gospel narratives. The servant is born, grows up disfigured and despised, suffers at the hands of his enemies, is put to death, and is exalted by God and distinguished afterwards in glorification. He shocked virtually everyone by his unsightly appearance, yet he bore this ignominy with silence and resolve. Who could have believed that God would choose to redeem humankind through such a seemingly disgusting agent? Who could have known that the Lord's great power could be manifested through weakness, sickness, and even death? And yet God boldly proclaims that a new thing has been done: God's servant suffered for *their* sins, not for *his* sins; and because of the suffering of this servant, God now accepts his creatures in a new way. In a similar, albeit extended narrative, the Synoptic Gospels present Jesus as having been born, having suffered both persecution and rejection, died at the hands of his enemies, and subsequently been resurrected by God. Through his suffering and death, we are now redeemed from our sin. Is this parallelism coincidental? I think not! To be certain, there were clearly other motivating influences prompting the evangelists to write their Gospels. The death of the apostles and the kerygmatic needs of the emerging church certainly played a role. Moreover, we are becoming increasingly aware of the rich mixture of Jewish and Hellenistic traditions that intertwine to fashion the moving mosaic of a suffering messiah.[2] The sources of these traditions are many and varied. Isaiah 53 is not the only Old Testament text that could have served as a "proof" for a suffering messiah. Also, Paul makes a somewhat different use of this Isaiah 52:13 passage in justifying his mission to the Gentiles. Nevertheless, it seems clear that Isaiah 52:13ff. played a major role in the early stages of Christianity by providing essential images and perhaps even a model for the interpretation of Jesus' life and for assessing its significance theologically.

Admittedly, there is nothing particularly new or original in these suggestions about the function of Isaiah 52:13ff. in the formation of the Gospel narrative.[3] Even so, it is important from time to time for biblical theologians to retrace their exegetical steps, to ask new questions, and to reexamine older assumptions in light of new methodologies. Considering the proposed significance of Isaiah 52:13ff. for the New Testament and for the early church, this review is all the more necessary. Hence, let us begin our examination of the function of the fourth Servant Song in the theology of the early Christian traditions with a brief exegetical review of the passage itself. Then we can trace the use of the passage and its motifs in Hellenistic and Palestinian Judaism of the first century. Third, we will describe the function of this passage in the New Testament. By tracing the use of this Scripture in later Jewish and early Christian thought, we can gain a sharper, more accurate insight into the way one particular Old Testament text functions in the New Testament.

Translation of the Text

Ordinarily, one would not begin a historical survey of a passage's function in later theology with an analysis of major problems in the translation of the text. However, because several important theological motifs from Isaiah 52:13ff. reflect particularly nuanced interpretations of textually problematic words and phrases, it seems necessary to identify and to discuss briefly the most important of these translation issues.

The Masoretic text (MT) of Isaiah 52:13–53:12 is corrupt in several places and contains difficult and ambiguous readings in other places.[4] In a word, the Hebrew text is not nearly as clear and straightforward as the *New Revised Standard Version* (NRSV) translation suggests. In Hebrew poetry, participial clauses, infinitives, nominal clauses, and gerundive clauses are difficult to translate even with a well-preserved text; when the text is corrupt, translation becomes next to impossible. And as any first-year student of a foreign language knows, when you cannot translate a word or phrase verbatim, you make an educated guess. Or, as we academics would argue, you make an interpretation! In two or three crucial places in the passage under consideration, interpretation is precisely what has occurred, particularly where the MT has suffered distortion or where textual dislocation has occurred.[5]

Some of these translation problems are minor and may be merely noted and bypassed for reasons of time. For example, in Isaiah 52:14a, the MT text reads "as many were appalled at "*you*." The Syriac version and several Targums changed the text to read "at *him*," making the pronominal suffix consistent with the third person masculine singular in verse 15a. Also, verse 14b is frequently relocated to 53:2, where the ugliness and despicable appearance of the servant is described. Grammatical consistency and logical clarity within the unit itself warrants these changes; even so, they have little bearing on the greater issues in theological interpretation.

In 52:15, the MT reads *yazzĕh*—"he shall sprinkle"— Hiphil, imperfect, third person masculine singular. The subject is implied—the servant—and the object is many nations. Some commentators suggest that this Hebrew word explains (or at least relates to) the astonishment of "many persons" in verse 14a.[6] The Septuagint (LXX), followed by the Old Latin version, changes the verb to *thaumázontai* so as to coincide with the parallelism of verse 14a and of verse 15a/b, thereby reversing the subject and the object. They read: "Many nations shall wonder at him." The NRSV makes the servant the subject of "startle." Although there is no Hebrew textual support for the LXX and Old Latin changes, verse 15b seems to warrant a surprising public reaction to the servant. Yet such logic does not always justify emendations. Perhaps as God's newly provided expiation for the sins of humankind the servant may well have cultically "sprinkled" many nations.

In 53:2, the third person masculine singular suffix is odd—*l'pānāw*"before him" (the implied antecedent is the Lord). Many translators emend the text to "before us," because the servant grew up before his peers, not before God. Paul Volz, following S. R. Driver, suggests dividing the Hebrew word and reading it "not comely."[7] Again, I choose to stay with the MT, because the servant did indeed grow up before the Lord, even if only in the figurative sense.

In 53:8, the nature of the servant's ordeal is unclear due to the ambiguity of the *min*-preformative. Christopher R. North suggests three possible interpretations introduced by *mē'osĕr*

(1) From imprisonment and from judgment, he was taken away; (2) By reason of an oppressive judgment, he was taken away; and (3) without hindrance and without judgment.[8]

North prefers the first option. *The New English Bible* (NEB) reads "without protection, without justice," which seems wholly unlikely.[9] I would propose taking the double *min*-preformatives in a comparative sense and translating as follows: "With more force than justice, he was taken away." I realize that the *min*-comparative *usually* requires the word tob, but Gesenius-Kautzsch-Cowley (GKC) cites a few instances where tob is absent.[10] Less clear, however, is the object of *lŭqqăḥ*—"he was taken away." To where and how? Was the servant removed for execution or for burial? Certainly, verse 8c suggests that he died, but how he died (execution or disease) remains unclear. Generally, commentators feel that the enemies of the servant executed him for some unnamed sin.[11] The final phrases of 53:8 are clearly corrupt and require considerable emendation. The antecedent of *ămmī* (my people) may either be the Lord or the speaker. Also, *negă'lāmō* (a plague [was] for him) is usually emended, following the LXX—"he went to his death." My own judgment is to read the entire verse as a summation by the speaker, who describes the vicarious atonement of the servant—"for the sin of my people, he was executed."

The reference in verse 9b to "in his death" b'mōtăw is difficult, for it breaks the parallelism with "his grave" (v. 9a). The LXX and the Syriac both emend to "his grave."

Because this change requires only minimal changes in MT, I can concur.

Verse 10 in the MT literally translates "It pleased YHWH to crush him, to make (him) sick." However, the LXX emends the text to read "the Lord was pleased to cleanse him from sickness." The Vulgate reads, "the Lord was pleased to crush him with sickness." North, following H. H. Rowley, reads, "But Yahweh was pleased to crush him with sickness, truly he gave himself as a guilt offering."[12] The NEB again proposed an even more radical change, "Yet the Lord took thought for his tortured servant and healed him who had made himself a sacrifice for sin."[13]

The second line of verse 10, although grammatically clear, is not easy to interpret: "He shall see his seed; his days are lengthened, and the Lord by his hand caused him (the servant) to succeed." More will be said on this verse later. Suffice it to note that interpreters must exercise caution in overinterpreting a difficult text. The basic point is that somehow the servant will watch his offspring grow, and that YHWH will grant him longevity. The specifics of this imagery are completely lacking, but Hebrew poetry, particularly in Second Isaiah, frequently communicates only in general images or pictures.

Verse 11a is likewise very difficult to interpret due to complex Hebrew syntax. Although the MT is clear, the syntax is not easy. Literally, it reads "From the turmoil of his soul, he shall see, he shall be satisfied." The NEB, following the Isaiah scroll from Qumran, reads, "After all his pains, he shall be bathed in light."[14] I would propose the following translation: "From the agony of his soul, he shall find satisfaction." Equally problematic is verse 11c: "On account of his knowledge, the righteous one my servant shall make righteous many persons" (MT). Allowing for dittography, North translates, "My servant shall bring justification to many."[15] This is reasonable, because dittography is not an unusual occurrence in Hebrew poetry.

The few translation issues mentioned here by no means exhaust the problems created by a defective and ofttimes obscure Hebrew text. Much more study needs to be made of the LXX text before conclusive translation decisions can be justified. However, on the basis of this brief survey, it should be clear at least that the translation of the fourth Servant Song is by no means clear and straightforward. The passage offers a veritable feast for interpreters. Several modern commentators and translators (NEB, ASV) have exercised great liberties with the *textus receptus*. Their translations clearly reflect christological assumptions evident in later New Testament uses of this passage; this is particularly true in 53:10, 11, 12. Also, it will be important to note later in this essay how certain textual emendations (some questionable) in this difficult passage have played major roles in the New Testament perception of the nature and mission of the servant. But for now we must move on to other matters.

Date and Authorship

A majority of modern commentators follow Bernhard Duhm's tripartite analysis of Isaiah: First Isaiah (1–39), Second Isaiah (40–55), and Third Isaiah (56–66). Further, they concur, for the most part, that Second Isaiah was an anonymous prophet who belongs somewhere toward the latter part of the Babylonian Exile. Internal evidence (45:1) suggests a time that follows Cyrus's conquests elsewhere in the ancient Near East, but not yet including Babylon. The restoration themes, the new exodus theme, and the hope for a second Temple all point to an exilic date for the bulk of chapters 40–55. Typical of most standard critical *Introductions*, Georg Fohrer proposes a date for Second Isaiah sometime between 550 and 538 B.C.E.[16]

Attempts to divide Second Isaiah's ministry into two or three separate periods are unconvincing due to (a) ambiguous historical references, (b) questionable translations, and (c) artificial divisions within the book itself.[17] This is not to say that one cannot identify separate literary units within the book that may or may not have belonged to the anonymous author—the Servant Songs are a case in point—but to assign early chapters (40–48) to a period prior to Cyrus's conquest in 539 B.C.E. and later chapters (49–55) to a time after Sheshbazaar's return in 538 B.C.E. is highly suspect. Even if it may be arguable to some scholars that Second Isaiah himself composed the fourth Servant Song, or whether he obtained it elsewhere, the life of this text must begin so far as we are concerned with its incorporation into its present exilic literary corpus. Its literary prehistory lies beyond our needs for the present study.

For Christopher North, the author of the fourth Servant Song is somewhat problematic due to a substantial number of words (46 in fact) that are entirely unique to this particular unit and found nowhere else in the book. He concludes nevertheless that the author is probably Second Isaiah himself.[18] He argues that "there is nothing in the language that is inconsistent with his authorship, and that the passage has definite points of contact with his writings, indeed more in common with his work than with any other writer known to us."[19] North also attributes the three other Servants Songs to Second Isaiah, noting nevertheless that the fourth song does seem different in many respects from the other three songs. For example, the nature of the servant's mission differs in 42:1–4, where Israel, God's servant, is to bring justice to the world. In 52:13—53:12, the servant, an individual, vicariously suffers for the sins of all humankind. Fohrer, however, suggests that the Servant Songs belong to a writer other than Second Isaiah.[20] Although Claus Westermann recognizes that the four Servant Songs represent a strand different from the main corpus of Second Isaiah, he does not doubt that the first three songs belong to the prophet himself; he is less certain who composed the fourth song, which assumes the servant's death.[21] (How could the servant report an account of his own suffering and death, particularly using verbs in the perfect and waw-consecutive imperfect tenses?) James Muilenberg, in *The Interpreter's Bible*, more emphatically than North argues that Second Isaiah wrote the fourth song and placed it strategically in its present position in his collection of songs.[22] Others suggest that this final poem derives from Third Isaiah (a disciple of Second Isaiah) and refers to the death and exaltation of Second Isaiah himself.[23] Sigmund Mowinckel circumvents the problem of authorship for the fourth Servant Song by suggesting that it is a matter of "subordinate interest."[24] Without committing academic heresy and dismissing a hitherto fundamental question of the historical-critical method, I must concur with Mowinckel, at least as far as the present study is concerned. The internal linguistic and literary evidence is too inconclusive to designate secondary authorship with anything like reasonable certainty. There are no historical references or anachronisms to suggest a later or earlier date of composition and of a different author. More substantively, the poetic techniques in this song, the theological theme of the song, plus the strategic and essential function of the place of this song in the book as a whole strongly suggest that this passage either belongs to or was redacted substantially by the author of the rest of Second Isaiah (so Roy F. Melugin, Aage Bentzen, and Bernhard W. Anderson).[25] To pursue these questions of authorship further would add little, if anything, to the present inquiry. Our efforts now must be directed toward describing the form and function of the fourth song in Second Isaiah as a whole.

Structure and Genre

The external structure of the fourth Servant Song falls naturally into two main parts: (1) a third person report on the earthly suffering and exaltation of the servant, which is (2) set within a larger framework of a divine speech proclaiming YHWH's ultimate vindication of his tortured and detestable servant.[26] The poem reflects at least two speakers: YHWH and an anonymous third person speaker or speakers (possibly a chorus or Israel). Admittedly, the inconsistent use of a third person singular and a third person plural speaker in the center section causes difficulties in interpretation. It is also clear that this third person narrator/s is/are neither the servant himself, nor is he the one who first witnessed the misery of the servant. A perspective of some distance from these experiences characterizes the entire center section; yet at the same time, the speaker knows full well that the servant's vicarious sacrifice was in fact made for *him* (them). "The Lord laid on him the sins of all of *us*" (v. 6b; cf. also v. 4a, 4b). The overall dramatic effect of the poem is heightened by the dialectical qualities of distance and intimacy—"him-us."[27] Similarly, the poet uses repetition for a more intense effect: "he was despised" (53:3a–3d); "he opened not his mouth" (53:7a–7e); "we had no regard for him" (53:3d–4c), and so forth. The highly sophisticated poetic style displayed in the fourth Servant Song attests to considerable literary skill. His techniques as a poet are as profound as his message is new.

The structure of this divine announcement may be outlined as follows:

I. Divine Announcement of Exaltation (52:13–15)
   A. Divine exaltation (53:13)
   B. Public surprise (53:14–15a,b)
      1. Perception of what they were not told (53:15c)
      2. Understanding of what they had not heard (53:15d)

II. An Account of the Servant's Suffering, Death, and Exaltation (53:1–11a)
   A. Introductory Rhetorical Questions (53:1)

B. The Early Life of the Servant (53:2, 3)
  1. Like a root from dry ground (53:2a)
  2. Extremely ugly and unsightly (53:2b)
  3. A man of sorrow
  4. Public rejection
C. The Atonement of the Servant (53:4–11)
  1. Misunderstanding of his suffering (v. 4b)
  2. True understanding, why he suffered (v. 5)
     (a) Bearing our sins
     (b) His chastisement made us whole (v. 6)
  3. His passive acceptance of his suffering (v. 7)
  4. His execution (v. 8)
  5. His death and burial (v. 9)
  6. His exaltation (vv. 10, 11a)

III. Divine Announcement of Exaltation (53:11b–12)

In his BZAW monograph *The Formation of Isaiah 40–55*, Roy Melugin identifies 52:13–53:12 as "two speeches of salvation, between which . . . is found a confession by the nations."[28] He correctly rejects Johannes Begrich's identification of the song as a psalm of thanksgiving, strongly influenced by the language of the lament psalm.[29] On the basis of the introduction and conclusion, the fourth Servant Song may be classified, form-critically, as a divine hymn, and it does certainly reverberate with YHWH's praise for his servant. But on closer inspection into the internal structure and form-critical composition of chapter 53, a variety of other elements appear. Precise identification, along Hermann Gunkel's lines, of the literary genre of the fourth Servant Song is complicated by the middle section of the song, 53:1–9. Begrich characterized this section as the heart of a psalm of thanksgiving, because the typical center of this genre is a narrative description of human travail and deliverance (Ps. 138; 73).[30] Mowinckel finds elements in Isaiah 53 of both the psalms of penitence and those of lament.[31] Further, Mowinckel suggests that the poet used elements of a funeral dirge to describe the death experience of the servant.[32] From a different point of view, Gerhard von Rad identifies the fourth Servant Song as a "prophetic liturgy."[33] He understands the poem as a type of liturgical proclamation, used in the second Temple to celebrate the atoning work of the servant. But because of the "dirge" character of the center section, the song goes far beyond what ordinarily could be expected in cultic celebration.[34] Here God's ultimate vindication of his humiliated servant provides an alternative to traditional sacrifice and offers to believers a compensatory form of expiation.

From this survey of form-critical analyses of the genre (or genres) of the fourth Servant Song, we may conclude that, although it shares many elements in common with other genres, it seems unique. Begrich correctly relates it to a psalm of thanksgiving, but nowhere in any members of this genre in the Old Testament does divine speech open or close such songs, nor does it even appear. Likewise, divine approval and vindication do not appear in individual psalms of lament—only expressions of hope and confidence. The funeral dirge occupies only a small section of the fourth Servant Song. In my judgment, von Rad's proposal that the song is a prophetic liturgy has some merit, or at least it explains many elements within a very complex unit. The cultic character of vicarious atonement is clearly affirmed in the death and exaltation of the servant. Unfortunately, von Rad cites no other examples of this genre elsewhere in Second Isaiah, nor anywhere else in the Old Testament.

Form-critically, the closest parallels to the fourth song are the other three Servant Songs in Second Isaiah: 42:1–4; 49:1–6; 50:4–9. Yet significant differences in internal structure exist among these four units, to say nothing of differences in the identity of YHWH's servant, the mission of this servant, and the theological significance of the servant. Nevertheless, they are all divine speeches celebrating the life and work of YHWH's servant. This genre-typicality transcends elements of particularity, at least as regards the broader issue of genre identification; hence, I would classify them as "Servant Songs"—a literary genre unique to Second Isaiah. A more precise form-critical identification must await further study.

Intention of the Fourth Song

Consistent with the preceding discussion of the structure and genre of the fourth Servant Song, the intention of 52:13–53:12 is twofold: (1) a divine proclamation of the glorification of the servant; and (2) an account of his ironic life and death as vicarious atonement. The song opens elegantly with a declaration of YHWH's intention (employing imperfect verbs) to exalt and to honor his servant. This act of glorification will give new meaning to the sense of amazement and shock exhibited by the many persons who knew and saw the servant humiliated. His earthly disfigurement and ignominious death were not at all as they seemed, that is, divine retribution for *his* sins! Now, as YHWH suggests, people will see what they had not been told, and they will understand what they had not heard. The suffering and death of this figure are to be understood from the standpoint of his exaltation following his death (from the end)—not from his earthly experience (the beginning and the middle). God was about to do a new thing—a glorious thing. One can sense the excitement and the joy over YHWH's vindication of his servant. The introduction and the conclusion are ablaze with the fires of celebration and anticipation. This mighty act of YHWH will be like none of his acts of old; it is a new, totally unique act!

The center section of the fourth Servant Song is a retrospective account of the servant's youth, his suffering, his death, and his burial. Scholarly opinions differ as to the identity of the speakers in the center section. In part, the confusion exists because certain references are third person masculine singular and others are third person

masculine plural. The most persuasive argument, to me
at least, is that the singular may be a "collective," referring to the community who witnessed the servant, and
who only *now* (following his exaltation by YHWH) realize
the atoning mission of his life.[35] The speakers lament
their ignorance and their lack of concern for the plight or
the execution of the tormented servant; but yet, as they
exclaim, "Who could believe what we have heard?"
There is a real sense of irony in the inevitable plan of
YHWH at work here; the Lord did not intend that they
should grasp the full significance of this new deed before
it was time. The Lord's divine will did, in fact, include
public disdain and execution of this servant. It is unclear
whether the speakers actually knew and witnessed first-
hand the servant or whether they are reporting a tradition
that has now been disclosed to them. Unlike customary
dirge accounts in the Old Testament, the speakers do not
describe the great renown in which the deceased had been
held, his incredible accomplishments, and his international
fame; instead, they focus on precisely the opposite. They
describe his utter wretchedness! He was physically gro-
tesque, ugly, and disfigured—not like a beautiful, green
tree, but like a scrubby, parched stem, sprung up in an
arid desert. He was ill and sickly. He had no social stand-
ing. He was utterly despised—a lonely, solitary individual
who stood apart from society. Surely, so they thought, this
man had sinned grievously, and he was experiencing the
Lord's just punishment. Finally he died, perhaps executed
at the hands of his enemies following condemnation for
some unspecified crime. He was buried among criminals
and outcasts and quickly forgotten. His misery and dis-
grace defiled and eradicated all memory of his wretched
life. Yet through all of this agony he remained silent, qui-
etly consenting to his miserable fate. Unlike Job or Jeremiah, he complained not once.

But this is not the end of the story. Now suddenly
something new has happened—something no less than a
miracle in the eyes of the speakers. The Lord has dis-

closed a new message to them concerning what, up until now, they have not known. This new truth is that the wretched suffering and death of the servant was not a consequence of *his* sin, but occurred precisely because of *their* sins! Moreover, his death has now been set aside, replaced by exaltation and glorification. And most important of all, because of his death, all persons now stand in a new relationship with the Lord. Because of the servant, God has removed their guilt. The servant has "purged them from their sins; he has born their transgression; his stripes have made them whole; he has poured his life for their sins," and so forth. He gave his life vicariously as a "sin offering" for them. He has made of himself a substitute offering for their sins. Now the speakers realize the irony of what has just occurred; they misunderstood the servant. God has revealed this new understanding to them through the glorification of his servant. The unit then concludes, as it began, with a divine speech concerning YHWH's exaltation of his servant.

Who, exactly, was this suffering and exalted servant? Of whom is the prophet speaking? As Christopher North has shown in his work *The Suffering Servant in Deutero-Isaiah*, this is not a question that yields an easy answer. He indicates that there are currently four theories that command respect:[36]

1. The servant was an anonymous prophet, contemporary with Second Isaiah, whom the prophet believed to be Israel's future messiah.

2. The servant was Deutero-Isaiah. Some argue that the fourth song was written by Third Isaiah, honoring his "martyred master."[37]

3. "Israel" is the servant.

4. The servant is a messianic prototype, an ideal figure modeled after the slain King Josiah.

Mowinckel presents a forceful case for rejecting both the poetical "personification" concept and the collectivist theory of identity. Against the view that the servant is Israel, Mowinckel suggests that no Old Testament prophet could say that Israel suffered innocently, or that she bore sufferings silently and patiently, or "least of all that her sufferings were incomprehensible."[38]

Of more recent vintage, two more positions have arisen that require our attention. Von Rad argues that because of the kind of extreme language used in the fourth song, the writer is not referring to an actual person; the servant refers to an "office" akin to that occupied by Israel's prophets.[39] Continuing, von Rad admits that Second Isaiah does apply this designation to Israel, but thinks that imposing it on Isaiah 53 raises too many insoluble problems.[40] Finally, von Rad indicates that the lines between the individual and the collective interpretations are "fluid at certain points."[41] There are points of cross connection between the two views.

A position similar to, but less ambivalent than, von Rad's is maintained by Bernhard Anderson, who argues in the fourth edition of his *Understanding the Old Testament*:

> It is unnecessary to choose between an individual and a corporate interpretation of the Servant of Yahweh, for both are true to the Israelite sense of community. The conception oscillates between the servant Israel and the personal servant who would perfectly fulfill Israel's mission. In his prophecy, the servant is a person, although no single person, past or contemporary corresponds completely to the type. For the person also includes and represents Israel, the community that is explicitly designated as Yahweh's servant.[42]

With regard to the fourth Servant Song, I think a case could be made that the "servant" is an enriched and embellished portrait of an actual individual. Whereas other songs clearly identify the servant as Israel, the fourth song may refer to Israel only theologically (and secondarily) as God's agent of revelation. Given natural Hebrew poetic liberty, the composer has idealized an anonymous figure and endowed him with attributes far exceeding the limits of actuality. Such a person probably served as a model for Second Isaiah's fourth song, but within the framework of poetic style this individual absorbed traits that elevated him to the category of the ideal. As the author of Second Isaiah used other oracles, hymns, and poems to celebrate his message, and as Israel's redemption from exile became imminent, he perceived a new sense of mission for God's chosen people that could best be compared to that of his idealized servant. Hence, the collective interpretation may have existed side by side with the individual interpretation within the context of the book.

A second exegetical issue to be addressed briefly is whether the author of Second Isaiah regarded the servant as messianic. As is well known, the term *messiah* in the Old Testament is a royal personage of the Davidic line who is destined by YHWH to usher in a new age of peace and justice (Isa. 7:10–17; 9:1–7; 11:1–9). He is an eschatological figure, quickened by the Lord's Spirit, who restores humanity to a prefall state. Through him YHWH continues to honor his everlasting covenant with David (2 Sam. 7:1–29). Second Isaiah alludes to this royal covenant (55:3–5), with the modification that it is to be made with the new Israel who respond to YHWH's call. Nowhere in his poems or songs does Second Isaiah announce the resumption of a royal Davidic line. In contrast to the messianic king, the servant is depicted as a weak, pathetic outcast. He has no power or authority. He has no enviable features. Most scholars conclude, therefore, that the composer of Second Isaiah does not identify the servant with the messiah.[43] Such an identification is to begin much later, during the first century. In the kerygmatic proclamation of the New Testament, Jesus, the messiah, assumed the role of the servant, suffered, died, was buried and exalted. In Jesus, the servant and the messiah merged!

LXX Translation of "Servant" in Second Isaiah

The Hebrew word *servant* 'ĕbĕḏ, can be found 807 times in the MT.[44] In the LXX, the following Greek words are used to translate 'ĕbĕḏ: *pais* (and derivatives) 340 times; *doulos* (and derivatives) 327 times; *oikĕtēs* 63 times; *therapōn* 46 times; and *huios* and *hupērĕtes* once each.[45] In the translation of the Isaiah 42:1–4 and 49:1–6 passages, *pais* refers to Israel and is hence a clear witness to early "collective" theories. With 52:13–53:12 in the LXX, however, *pais* more likely refers to an individual figure.[46] Because the LXX renders *yōnēq* by *paidion* (familiar from the "messianic" text in Isa. 9:6), Walther Zimmerli and Joachim Jeremias suggest that the translators of the LXX clearly viewed the servant as a messianic figure.[47] Further, he is a figure who has not yet come, but whose appearance is awaited with great hopes—as evidenced by a change in verb tense from perfect (MT) to future (LXX) in 52:14ff.[48] Likewise, the servant's humiliation and rejection are also translated using future tenses in the LXX. Thus, interpretations of the servant in Isaiah 52:13–53:12 among Greek-speaking Jews are clearly messianic and futuristic, unlike in the Old Testament. Whether suffering was understood as an aspect of messianism among Greek-speaking Jews is another question altogether. When this new interpretation of the servant as messianic first penetrated Jewish thought has not yet been determined. It obviously occurred sometime between 540 B.C.E. (Second Isaiah) and the late third century B.C.E. (LXX). Also, it seems clear that the nature and status of the office of "messiah" had likewise lost its royal aspects.

Both Reginald Fuller, in *The Foundations of New Testament Christology*, and Morna D. Hooker, in *Jesus and the Servant*, reject the position that the servant was messianic in the LXX.[49] In fact, they argue that Jeremias bases his entire argument for the messianic character of Isaiah 53 in the Greek translations of the Old Testament on a paucity

of sources, and even then, on sources that have a distinc-
tively Christian bias (Aquila and Theodotian).[50] Of
course, these two early writers identify the messiah with
the servant, but this identification is late first century and
is post-Pauline. Edward Lohse is another dissenting voice
from Jeremias's thesis that anti-Christian polemics
prompted Targum interpretations of Isaiah 53 to transfer
the notion of suffering from the "servant" (or the messiah) to either Israel or to other nations.[51] He argues that
"the atoning power of vicarious suffering was very widespread in 1st Century Judaism, yet Isaiah 53 was *never*
adduced in support of it."[52] So some question exists as to
whether the Greek-speaking Jews included suffering as
part of the role of the messiah.

   Pais theou occurs rarely in late Jewish literature after
100 B.C.E.[53] In fact, as Jeremias argues, the title seems to
have fallen out of use altogether as a messianic referent,
except in Old Testament quotations. In one set of Hellenistic Jewish writings, the term *servant*, now translated by
pais, means only "child." Jeremias suggests that continued use of *pais* in this sense disassociated the term from
its prophetic roots and eventually assumed a more general meaning as a "righteous person" (Wisd. of Sol.
2:13).[54]

   On the other hand, the term *pais theou*, meaning "servant" (not child) of God is used in later Judaism of the
first century to identify several types of persons or
groups: (1) a self-description of the worshiper;[55] (2) a collective reference to Israel (singular and plural);[56] (3) a title
of honor for special, divine appointments or special
groups;[57] (4) a designation for the messiah.[58] In the Old
Testament, the messiah is designated as "my servant"
specifically only five times: in Ezekiel 34:23f.; 37:24f.; and
Zechariah 3:8.[59] In later Jewish writings, it appears in 4
Ezra, and in Targums on Isaiah, Zechariah, and Ezekiel.
Apart from quotations, this designation is curiously
absent from the rabbinic literature. Thus, Zimmerli and
Jeremias conclude, " 'Servant of God' as a real title for the

Messiah never existed in Judaism, apart from quotations, as is shown by its restriction to divine discourse."[60]

After the beginning of the second century, "servant of God" became translated as *doulos* rather than as *pais* because the latter term had acquired nuances of "child of God" rather than "servant."[61] Also, Hellenistic Judaism favored the collective interpretations of the Second-Isaiah servant.[62] But Fuller argues that Jeremias's evidence is too limited; actually, he argues, "where the theme of vicarious atonement is taken up from Isaiah 53, we have to suspect a Palestinian, rather than a Hellenistic provenance."[63]

The Function of the Fourth Servant Song in NT Christology

According to Jeremias, there are only a few New Testament passages that use a specific word or phrase taken from the fourth Servant Song and used in reference to Jesus.[64] In Matthew 8:17, the evangelist reports that Jesus cast out spirits and healed the sick in order to fulfill Isaiah's prophecy "He took our infirmities and bore our diseases." In Luke 22:37, Jesus anticipates his own death among sinners, "in accordance with Scripture" (Isa. 53:12). In John, popular unbelief in Jesus was not mere credulity; it was that Isaiah's Scripture might be fulfilled: "Lord, who has believed our report and to whom has the arm of the Lord been revealed" (Isa. 53:1). In Acts 8:32ff., Phillip teaches the Ethiopian eunuch about Jesus being the messiah by explaining the passage from Isaiah 53:7ff.: "As a sheep led to the slaughter," and so forth. Finally, in Romans 15:21, Paul legitimates his plans to preach the gospel in new and distant lands, in accordance with Isaiah 52:15: "They shall see who have never been told of him," and so forth. Except for Paul, who uses the servant text to justify his future mission to new lands, all direct quotations in the New Testament from the fourth Servant

Song validate the claim that, in one respect or another, Jesus' life and ministry had been announced in the Old Testament and was now fulfilled. Note, however, that none of these direct references to Isaiah 53 relate to Jesus' ultimate atoning significance as the one who suffered and died for the sins of many. For the interpretation of Jesus as the vicariously atoning servant in Isaiah, we must look elsewhere to indirect, but nonetheless unmistakable, references. It is clear, however, from examining these references that the early traditions used the Old Testament as predictive of events that they believed had been fulfilled in the life of Jesus. The same hermeneutical principle is at work in the New Testament as was at work earlier in the fourth Servant Song itself; a proper understanding of certain events can be made only from the end, not from the beginning, that is, from an eschatological point of view. The servant was not understood (he was misunderstood, in fact) until his postdeath exaltation. Similarly, only in the resurrection faith could Jesus' own life be assessed properly.

From material that may be considered as "pre-Pauline" tradition,[65] 1 Corinthians 15:3–5 reports that "Christ died for our sins in accordance with the scriptures." Clearly, what Paul received by way of this tradition was an interpretation of Christ's death that found in the fourth Servant Song an ideal prototype for vicarious atonement. Just as had the servant in Isaiah 53, Christ died for our sins (Isa. 53:4–6). As the servant had been exalted by God, Christ was raised from the dead (Isa. 53:10–11). In Romans 4:25, Paul again cites a tradition that understands Jesus' death and resurrection in light of Isaiah 53: "Who was put to death for our trespasses and raised for our justification." In the important christological hymn found in Philippians 2:6–11, Paul probably has the Isaiah-servant in mind when he describes how Christ lowered himself to assume the human form of a servant, obediently suffered humiliation, even to death, and was subsequently exalted by God. Clearly, the early christological traditions used by Paul in his writings made extensive use of the fourth Servant Song to interpret soteriologically the suffering, death, and resurrection of Christ. The Philippian hymn (2:6–11) is particularly significant in that both Christ's life and that of the servant follow the same general sequence: birth (and/or early life), suffering, humiliation, death, exaltation-resurrection. At very early stages of Christology, the servant of the fourth Servant Song furnished not only a chronological sequence but a theological model for understanding (and proclaiming) Jesus as the Christ. Similarly, argues Jeremias, presynoptic traditions make use of the fourth Servant Song.[66] Jeremias finds allusions to Isaiah 53 in ancient eucharistic formulae, which stand behind texts such as Mark 14:24.[67] The *lutron* saying (Mark 10:45; Matt. 20:28) also seems to reflect Isaiah 53. In fact, he argues, Mark 9:12 and Luke 22:37 indicate that in the presynoptic traditions used by all three Gospels, when Jesus cites Scripture in regard to his passion, Isaiah 53 stands in the background.[68] As with the pre-Pauline traditions, Isaiah 52:13–53:12 furnishes the framers of early presynoptic Christology an important paradigm with which to interpret Jesus. Also, the eucharistic formulations, at least to Jeremias, seem to depend on vicarious atonement imagery displayed in Isaiah 53. The constant liturgical celebration reminded them that Christ died for our sin.

The Gospel of John also makes use of an early tradition interpreting Christ in light of Isaiah 53.[69] The Good Shepherd (John 10:7–18) who lays down his life for his sheep seems reminiscent of the suffering servant. John 16:32 reflects an allusion to Isaiah 53:6, in turning ("scattering") to our own way. Clearly, John 12:38 uses Isaiah 53:1 in reference to the predetermined unbelief of the Jews. Just as the speakers in Isaiah 53:6 admitted to a misunderstanding of the servant's suffering (where, in actuality, the Lord willed that they *should* not understand), so also in John the unbelief of the Jews was not accidental. It is interesting that John makes no references to Jesus' suffering as a fulfillment of Isaiah's prophecies. One must wonder whether John's early christological materials were the same as those materials used by the Synoptics and by Paul.

To summarize, the great majority of references to Isaiah 53, both directly and indirectly, belong to very early stages in the New Testament traditions. Paul and the writers of the Synoptics employ christological traditions and formulations that outline Jesus' life and interpret Christ's vicarious suffering in light of the servant prototype in Isaiah 52:13–53:12. The death both of Jesus and of the humiliated one are counterbalanced by their exaltation to glory. Although the Isaiah servant was not described as being resurrected, he was nonetheless exalted by God and glorified before men. In the very earliest days, even before the letters of Paul, to say nothing of the oral tradition preceding the Gospels, the early church used the Old Testament as predictions and proofs of events that just occurred or were about to occur. Isaiah 53 certainly must have been a favorite text, for it supplied both a chronological parallel and a theological model with which to interpret Jesus' suffering and death. Furthermore, Isaiah 53 explained other events in Jesus' life: healings (Matt. 12:18–20), Israel's unbelief (John 12:8), and so forth. Finally, Paul uses Isaiah 53 to justify his missionary journey.

A second set of New Testament texts using verses from Isaiah 52:13–53:12 are those in which Jesus refers to himself (or supposedly so) as the suffering servant.[70] In Mark 9:12, Jesus predicts that he is to suffer many things and be treated with contempt (Isa. 53:3, nibzeh). References to his imminent death in Mark 9:31; 10:33; 14:21, Matt. 26:2, and Luke 24:7 all seem to have Isaiah 53:56 in mind. Oscar Cullman argues that "Jesus became conscious at the moment of his baptism that he had to take upon himself the *ebed Yahweh* role."[71] Reginald Fuller, on the other hand, doubts that Jesus ever used the term *servant* as a self-designation.[72] Continuing Fuller's argument, an examination of Jesus' understanding of his baptism indicates that, through his baptism by John, Jesus considered himself to have "crossed over into the proleptic presence of the age to come."[73] Yet Fuller disallows the "original Palestinian" form of baptism to infer Jesus' identification with the suffering, atoning servant of Isaiah 53.[74] In fact, as Heinz E. Tödt argues, the concept of "suffering for many" arose not from Isaiah 53, but from another source or tradition.[75] Tödt, in Fuller's judgment, destroys all notions that Jesus' self-understanding included the servant of the Lord, and even less did Jesus understand himself as the suffering servant of Isaiah 53.[76] Despite Tödt's argument, Fuller remains unconvinced.

Given the enormous amount of scholarly debate over the matter of Jesus' self-consciousness (or for that matter, over how we might know exactly anything that Jesus thought, said, or did), it is very difficult to describe Jesus' own use of the Old Testament, or more especially of Isaiah 52:13–53:12, with reference to himself. Even though the nature of the early pre-Gospel, pre-Pauline traditions is vague, there does seem to be some scholarly agreement as to the functions of our text in quotations, as described earlier.

To conclude this discussion of the place and function of Isaiah 53 in the New Testament, it is appropriate to examine very briefly two passages that provide insight on this matter. Up until recently, New Testament scholars understood Mark 10:45b to reflect the servant and substitutionary ransom theme in Isaiah 53. The text reads: "For the Son of Man came not to be served but to serve, and to give his life a ransom (lutron) for many" Mark 10:45, NRSV).

Many modern commentators assign this verse to an early Gospel tradition that Mark appropriated. Jesus' suffering and death were closely linked to soteriological motifs associated with the Son of Man. Just as does 1 Corinthians 15:3, this verse from Mark may have belonged to a Palestinian Jewish tradition.[77] Fuller, how-

ever, questions this source analysis and proposes instead
that the soteriological motif referred back to Psalm 118:22
and was not part of the earliest Son of Man tradition.
Such a motif could have arisen from "the general idea of
the atoning significance of the death of martyrs."[78] No
other Son of Man sayings (except here) refer to the atoning significance of Jesus' death. Later perhaps, Fuller suggests, in the eucharistic tradition of the church, the
soteriological motif was added to the Son of Man traditions.[79]

Vincent Taylor, in his commentary on Mark, suggests
that the verse is genuine with Mark, and that lutron is
used metaphorically, not literally.[80] Other scholars, he
notes, assign the verse to Pauline circles, because Christ's
death is central to Paul's theology. Whether this saying is
authentic to Mark, or whether he employed a preexistent
tradition (Pauline or not), the thrust of the lutron is that
Christ's atoning sacrifice was viewed as a "ransom" for
human sinfulness. This is precisely the soteriological significance of the servant in Isaiah 53.

The other great passage displaying Isaiah 53 in its
background is Philippians 2:6–11. Generally, it is
considered to be a liturgical hymn, of pre-Pauline origin.
It too is held to have belonged to the early Palestinian
tradition. Specifically, the hymn relates to Isaiah 53 in
several phrases: (1) "emptied himself" (v. 7) parallels
Isaiah 53:12c; (2) servant, doulos (v. 7) parallels Isaiah
53; (3) verse 9—"highly exalted him"—parallels Isaiah
53.[81] Fuller proposes on the other hand that the hymn is
a "product of Hellenistic Jewish Christian missionaries
working in a mainly Hellenistic gentile environment."[82]
The phrase morphēn doulou (form of a slave) relates not
to Isaiah 53, but to the "mythological conception of
man under the thralldom of the powers."[83] Few
commentators concur with Fuller's judgment, choosing
instead to view Isaiah 53 as the background for parts of
this hymn.

Conclusion

By using form-critical analysis, we characterized Isaiah 52:13–53:12 as a Servant Song, that is, a divine speech celebrating the accomplishments of the Lord's servant. The center section of this song is a choral narration of the tragic life and death of the Lord's servant, and of his subsequent exaltation. The unit functioned as endorsement of a new relationship between YHWH and his people, in which a substitutionary offering atoned for their sins. In the chorus, a new understanding of the suffering and death of the servant emerged as an important hermeneutical principle: certain events must be interpreted from the end rather than at the beginning or as they develop.

The LXX most frequently translated *'ebêd* as *pais* or *doulos;* of more importance, the Jewish translators began linking the servant concept with the messiah concepts and projecting this idealized figure into the future. It is unclear whether suffering was part of this synthesis of servant and messiah. In later Jewish writings, including many of the Targums, the servant motif became absorbed into the eschatological Son of Man in quotations from earlier prophetic writings.

In the New Testament, Isaiah 53 functions in several ways. It serves as a chronological model to sequence Jesus' life as parallel with the servant: birth or early life, suffering and earthly humiliation, death, burial and exaltation. Given the complex traditions from which the early Gospels emerged, I do not think Isaiah 53 was the only source for this chronological reconstruction, but it certainly played a role, and not an insignificant role at that. Also, Isaiah 53 seems to be cited often, or stand in the theological background, for the ransom aspect of Christian soteriology. Jesus (like the servant) died as a ransom for the sins of many.

In view of these considerations, the fourth Servant Song functions in at least four ways in the New Testament:

1. As a proof text justifying (a) certain actions of Jesus, (b) certain behavior of the Jews who failed to recognize him as the messiah, (c) early Christian eucharistic theology, and (d) Christian soteriological terminology.

2. As a concrete simile explaining the reality of Jesus' human suffering. Just as did the suffering servant, Christ Jesus assumed full humanity, suffered, and experienced earthly rejection, in accordance with God's fore-announced plan.

3. As both the source and authority for God's message of universal redemption—good news that was to be proclaimed in far and distant lands.

4. As a hermeneutical precedent for an eschatological interpretation of history, that is, from the end of time rather than at its beginning.

Jesus Christ, who by his suffering, death, and resurrection made a full and sufficient sacrifice for the sins of the whole world, truly lived (or perhaps relived) the experience of Second Isaiah's servant of the Lord.

Notes

1. Cf. Bernhard W. Anderson, ed., *The Old Testament and Christian Faith* (New York: Harper & Row, 1963). Although originally published in 1963, the articles in this volume mark a starting point for contemporary reflections on this issue. Some articles were written much earlier. For a broader discussion of OT/NT relationships, see Claus Westermann, ed., *Essays on Old Testament Hermeneutics*, trans. James L. Mays (Richmond: John Knox Press, 1963). See also James M. Efird, ed., *The Use of the Old Testament in the New and Other Essays* (Durham, N.C.: Duke University Press, 1972).

2. Cf. particularly James H. Charlesworth, *Jesus Within Judaism: New Light from Existing Archaelogical Discoveries* (New

York: Doubleday, 1988). Cf. Hugh Anderson, *Jesus and Christian Origins* (New York: Oxford University Press, 1964).

3. Several scholars have suggested this connection in general, but few, if any, have substantiated exegetically the proposal that Isaiah 53:13ff. functioned as such a model. Cf. Walther Zimmerli and Joachim Jeremias, *The Servant of God* ("Studies in Biblical Theology," no. 20, rev. ed.; London: SCM Press, 1965); Christopher R. North, *The Suffering Servant in Deutero-Isaiah*, 2d ed. (Oxford: Oxford University Press, 1956, 1963).

4. The Hebrew text for this translation is based on *Biblia Hebraica Stuttgartensia*, ed. Kurt Elliger & Wilhelm Rudolph (Stuttgart: Deutsche Bibelgesellschaft, 1984).

5. In dealing with textual and translation problems, I found the following sources helpful: Claus Westermann, *Isaiah 40–66*, (Philadelphia: Westminster Press, 1969), 253–255; cf. also North, *Suffering Servant*, 121–127.

6. North, *Suffering Servant*, 123.

7. Ibid., 123. Cf. also Westermann, *Isaiah 40–66*, 261.

8. North, *Suffering Servant*, 124–125.

9. *The New English Bible: Old Testament* (Oxford: Oxford University Press, 1970), 1036.

10. Kautzsch, E., *Gesenius' Hebrew Grammar*, trans. A. E. Cauley, 2d ed. (Oxford: Clarendon Press, 1910), 429–432.

11. North, *Suffering Servant*, 125. Cf. also Westermann, *Isaiah 40–66*, 265.

12. North, *Suffering Servant*, 126.

13. NEB, 1036.

14. Ibid.

15. North, *Suffering Servant*, 126. Cf. also Westermann, *Isaiah 40–66*, 255.

16. Georg Fohrer, *Introduction to the Old Testament*, trans. David E. Green (New York and Nashville: Abingdon Press, 1968), 375.

17. Contra Fohrer, *Introduction*, 376. Cf. also North, *Suffering Servant*, 178.

18. North, *Suffering Servant*, 169–177.

19. Ibid., 177.

20. Fohrer, *Introduction*, 380–381. For an excellent discussion of earlier views on the authorship of the songs, cf. Otto Eissfeldt, *The Old Testament: An Introduction*, trans. Peter R. Ackroyd (New York: Harper & Row, 1965), 333–334.

21. Westermann, *Isaiah 40–66*, 29.

22. James Muilenberg, "Isaiah 40–66," *The Interpreter's Bible* 5:422–776.

23. Kurt Elliger, *Deuterojesaya in seinern Verhältnis zu Tritojesaya*, 1933, as cited by North, *Suffering Servant*, 173–175.

24. Sigmund Mowinckel, *He That Cometh*, trans. Gerhard W. Anderson (New York and Nashville: Abingdon Press, 1954), 188–189.

25. Roy F. Melugin, *The Formation of Isaiah 40–55* (Berlin and New York: Walter de Gruyter, 1976), 74; Aage Bentzen, *Introduction to the Old Testament*, 2 vols. (Copenhagen: G. E. C. Gad, 1957), 110–111; Bernhard W. Anderson, *Understanding the Old Testament*, 4th ed. (Englewood Cliffs, N.J.: Prentice-Hall, 1986), 472–502.

26. Melugin, *Formation*, 73. Cf. also Johannes Begrich, *Studien zu Deuterojesajaesja* (rev. 1963), *BZAW* 25 (1938): 63–64.

27. Muilenberg, "Isaiah," *IB* 5:614–615.

28. Melugin, *Formation*, 167.

29. Ibid., 74.

30. As cited by Muilenberg, "Isaiah," *IB* 5:614.

31. Mowinckel, *He That Cometh*, 203.

32. Ibid.

33. Gerhard von Rad, *Old Testament Theology*, vol. 2, trans. D. M. C. Stalker (New York: Harper & Row, 1965), 255.

34. von Rad, *Old Testament Theology* 2:256.

35. North, *Suffering Servant*, 150–151.

36. Ibid., 194–201.

37. Ibid., 195.

38. Mowinckel, *He That Cometh*, 214.

39. von Rad, *Old Testament Theology* 2:258.

40. Ibid., 259.

41. Ibid., 260.

42. Anderson, *Understanding the Old Testament*, 494.

43. North, *Suffering Servant*, 218.

44. Walther Zimmerli and Joachim Jeremias, *The Servant of God*, ("Studies in Biblical Theology," no. 20, rev. ed.; Naperville, Ill.: Alec R. Allenson, 1965), 37.

45. Zimmerli and Jeremias, *Servant*, 37.

46. Ibid., 43.

47. Ibid.

48. Ibid.

49. Reginald H. Fuller, *The Foundations of New Testament Christology* (New York: Charles Scribner's Sons, 1965), 45; M. D. Hooker, *Jesus and the Servant* (London: SPCK, 1959), 55f.

50. Fuller, *New Testament Christology*, 45; Hooker, *Jesus*, 57.

51. Lohse, as cited by Fuller, *New Testament Christology*, 45.

52. Ibid.

53. Zimmerli and Jeremias, *Servant*, 45.
54. Ibid., 46–47.
55. Ibid., 47.
56. Ibid., 49.
57. Ibid., 48–51.
58. Ibid., 51–52.
59. Ibid., 51.
60. Ibid., 51–52.
61. Ibid., 53.
62. Ibid., 54–55.
63. Fuller, *New Testament Christology*, 66.
64. Zimmerli and Jeremias, *Servant*, 88.
65. Ibid.
66. Ibid., 90.
67. Ibid.
68. Ibid., 90–91.
69. Ibid., 92.
70. Ibid., 99ff.
71. Cullman, as cited by Fuller, *New Testament Christology*, 115–116.
72. Fuller, *New Testament Christology*, 117.
73. Ibid.
74. Ibid.
75. Tödt, as cited by Fuller, *New Testament Christology*, 118.
76. Fuller, *New Testament Christology*, 118–119.
77. Ibid., 153.
78. Ibid.
79. Ibid., 153–155.
80. Vincent Taylor, *The Gospel According to St. Mark*, 2d ed. (New York: St. Martin's Press, 1966), 443–445.
81. Fuller, *New Testament Christology*, 204–214.
82. Ibid., 206.
83. Ibid., 210.

INDEX OF SUBJECTS
AND AUTHORS